THE MISSIONARY MOVEMENT
FROM BRITAIN
IN MODERN HISTORY

THE MISSIONARY MOVEMENT
FROM BRITAIN
IN MODERN HISTORY

MAX WARREN
Canon of Westminster

SCM PRESS LTD
BLOOMSBURY STREET LONDON

To
ROSEMARY
GREGORY & TIMOTHY
and their share in the
Christian mission

FIRST PUBLISHED 1965
© SCM PRESS LTD 1965
PRINTED IN GREAT BRITAIN BY
NORTHUMBERLAND PRESS LTD
GATESHEAD

CONTENTS

PREFACE

The chapters in this book first took shape as a course of lectures given at the invitation of the Faculty of Divinity of Cambridge University during the Michaelmas term, 1964. To the Chairman and members of the Faculty Board I would express my deep appreciation for the honour they did me in extending this invitation.

In footnotes and in bibliography I have tried to indicate my main sources. But indebtedness can never be accurately measured by such devices. I would like, in particular, to express my obligation to six persons whose writings on similar subjects have stimulated my own studies—Dr Kenneth Cragg, Mr Philip Mason, Dr Roland Oliver, Miss Margery Perham, Dr John V. Taylor and Canon Douglas Webster.

In private duty bound I must also thank Wendy Bayliss, Judith Bowyer and Elizabeth Clay for their labours in reducing my handwriting to legibility.

M.A.C.W.

INTRODUCTION

Missions in History

THE Church in history has often succeeded in modifying her environment: she has always been modified by it. That is an historical judgement about the empirical Church, which is as true of the Church in its missionary outreach as it is of its institutional life. This book is about that missionary outreach from Britain as it can be traced in modern history from the eighteenth century until today. The environment within which the missionary movement is here studied is certainly political and economic. But it is more than that, it is social. And by 'social' I would be understood to mean that whole complex of inter-relationships which is the subject-matter of social anthropology.

This is in no way to underestimate the distinctively religious aspect of 'Missions': nor does it qualify the spiritual dedication of those who, either as missionaries or as their partners in prayer and support, have given themselves to this obedience. Spiritual dedication is not susceptible of definition. No more, be it added, is it immune from historical criticism. Saints, just because they are also sinners, are sometimes extremely silly. Yet we do well to pause before we allow the silliness of a saint to discount his sanctity. What is true of saints is true also of missionaries. Undoubtedly some missionaries have been saints. All, however, would be very willing to settle for a very much humbler designation. No less certainly, many of them appear to have been remarkably silly, at least by the world's standards

of sanity. Yet any serious student of modern history must find
some explanation of the missionary expansion of the Christian
Church. For the missionary has been an omnipresent factor in
modern history, either by his own presence or sometimes even
by the threat of that presence, as the following pages will help
to show. There is a nice touch of irony in the verdict of an
early missionary on his kind, which time has not invalidated:

> Honour and dishonour, praise and blame, are alike our lot:
> we are the impostors who speak the truth, the unknown men
> whom all men know; dying we still live on; disciplined by suffer-
> ing, we are not done to death; in our sorrows we have always
> cause for joy; poor ourselves, we bring wealth to many; penniless,
> we own the world.[1]

By the standards of big business or the resources available
to national governments that ancient boast has more in it of
meiosis than of hyperbole.

Yet this strange historical phenomenon cannot be accurately
appraised unless it be seen as integral to the political, economic
and social conditions of its time, even if we may claim that its
final meaning cannot be exhausted by any of these singly or by
all together. Nevertheless there is a need for a new approach to
the study of Missions, one which will view the whole enterprise
within its historic setting, registering the interplay of all the forces that go to determine human action. This will certainly provide a new look for many aspects of the missionary enterprise, a
recasting of some traditional estimates. But the Christian least
of all need be afraid of the results of a new look. Aware of the
'iniquity of our most holy things'[2] he will not expect the record of the missionary movement to be without plenty of
evidence of folly and sin. He will encourage himself nevertheless in the faith he shares with St Paul that God 'has chosen
things low and contemptible, mere nothings, to overthrow the
existing order', and he is more than ready to assent to what

[1] II Cor. 6.8-10 N.E.B.   [2] Exodus 28.38.

the Apostle affirms when he adds, 'And so there is no place for human pride in the presence of God.'[3]

The argument of this book is that there is a place for such a study side by side with the many valuable essays which seek to establish the biblical basis for mission, as well as those which offer a contemporary theology of mission. Indeed, a combination of these three would seem to offer a way forward to the discovery of what is to be the distinctive practice of mission in the new world that is coming to be. Each of these three fundamental approaches—the biblical, the theological and the environmental—has its own justification. But none is complete without the other. Recognizing that incompleteness is inescapable in any particular study, what follows is an attempt to understand the modern missionary movement in its historical context, to view it as a part of modern history.

Sources for Missionary History

A word must be said about the sources available for such a study, or to be more accurate for the innumerable studies that will be demanded if justice is to be done to so vast a theme.

I have suggested that 'the missionary has been an omnipresent factor in modern history, either by his own presence, or sometimes even by the threat of that presence'. Documentation of such a claim will have to be sought in parliamentary speeches, in blue books and white papers, in the archives of the Foreign Office, of the Colonial Office, of the Admiralty, in the biographies of statesmen and overseas governors. Nor must the term 'missionary' be too narrowly defined. When a statesman declaims about Britain's role as a propagator of 'Christianity and civilization', as during a large part of the modern period statesmen frequently did, this cannot just be dismissed as a typical piece of hypocrisy. Sometimes, strangely enough,

[3] I Cor. 1.28-29. N.E.B.

the statesman was quite sincere. But even supposing he was 'playing to the gallery' the fact that there was a gallery to welcome such 'play' is a fact of historical importance. Of whom was the gallery composed? We easily forget that throughout the nineteenth century the newspapers carried very full reporting of parliamentary debates. And there was an eager public to read them. The campaign for the abolition of slavery introduced a wholly new technique into political agitation,[4] and that technique of public meetings, petitions to Parliament, and extensive pamphleteering both expressed and nourished a newly awakened national conscience. That was the gallery to which statesmen had to play. Whether our generation finds it congenial or not, the fact remains that during the latter part of the eighteenth and throughout most of the nineteenth century it was as much a political axiom as it was a religious conviction that 'Christianity and civilization' were two sides of the same coin. The politician who so declaimed was appealing to a nation's conscience even when he was exploiting it for unworthy ends. And the missionary very easily became one symbol of the nation's conscience. From the point of view of historical evidence the exasperation of the official mind with interfering missionaries, and with such a powerful pressure group as Exeter Hall, is just as important as those public tributes to missions and missionaries which the publicity of missionary societies has not failed to note.

Here there is a field of research which may yet yield material for some new assessments, both of the course of general history and of the particular history of the Christian Church.

Another source for the study of the missionary movement in modern history, still far from adequately or systematically explored, is to be found in the literature of, or that dealing with, the resurgence of the great ethnic religions. The Brahmo

[4] See G. M. Trevelyan, *English Social History* (Longmans, Green, 1942), pp. 496-7.

Samaj, and the Arya Samaj, and the Ramakrishna Mission in Hinduism; the Ahmadiyyah movement in Islam, and the story of the Arab awakening; the syncretistic 'new' religions of Japan, and such movements as Baha'ism; all are eloquent of the impact of the Christian missionary movement.

Somewhere, presumably, a vast mass of information about the modern nationalist movements in Asia and Africa is also slowly accumulating waiting for an army of future scholars to study its origins. We know enough already to affirm that one of the more constructive influences which started this ferment was the 'omnipresent missionary'. He may not have willed the ferment consciously, but his very presence and the ideas he proclaimed helped to provoke it. In this connection it is interesting to read the record of the debates on the East India Company's Charter when it came up for review in 1793, in 1813 and in 1833. There were plenty of voices to insist that the entrance of missionaries into India would be the end of the British Raj in India. And plenty of voices were eagerly raised in rebuttal of such a charge. Which were right? Perhaps a balanced verdict would say that both were right and both were wrong! 'Though the mills of God grind slowly, yet they grind exceeding small'!

Meanwhile, in addition to all these sources of a general character, there are the huge quarries of research material provided by the archives of the missionary societies. These are slowly being explored today, but the exploration has only begun. What is so often forgotten in regard to such material is that even though it once provided the basis for official histories of the societies or for the biographies of missionaries this does not mean that the sources have been exhausted. The historians of any generation, and likewise the biographers, ask of their sources the questions in which they and their contemporaries are interested. The researchers of today and tomorrow will ask quite different questions and perhaps present us with some very different conclusions and a wholly new style of portrait. Supplementary to these sources are the archives of Lambeth Palace, which may yet yield a great deal of intriguing material about the role played in the modern missionary movement by the successors of Augustine of Canterbury.

I have been concerned here to indicate source material for research, primarily directed towards a fuller understanding of the missionary movement from Britain in modern times. In conclusion I would emphasize the strict limitations of what I have written above, and the no less strict limitations of the approach outlined in the succeeding chapters. The words 'from Britain' in the title are explicit. Yet even they are far too ambitious unless it be accepted that what has been attempted is no more than an outline sketch. Even the bibliography, though wide-ranging, is no more than an indication of some of the compass that needs to be boxed.

When it comes to the wider field of the Christian missionary enterprise in modern times, there is, I believe, a need for a number of studies which will deal from the same perspective with the missionary outreach of the Churches of Continental Protestantism, and with those of North America. And I would express the hope that someone who combines a firm attachment to the insights of the Reformation and an equal attachment to the cause of Christian unity might attempt a study of the missionary movement of the Roman Catholic Church from the reign of Pius IX to that of John XXIII, specializing, for example, in those missionary initiatives which have derived from France. If I have proposed a Protestant for this task it is not from any doubt of the ability of Roman Catholic historians, but because it is still true that a Protestant historian, writing on such a theme, will probably do more to educate Protestants in the real significance and inwardness of the missionary movement of the Roman Catholic Church than could even one of the modern missionary prophets of

Louvain's annual *Semaine de Missiologie*. The important thing, however, is that the work should be done, and that it be made available in English.

I would express this further hope and that is that some individual, or institution, with imagination would arrange for the treasures of missionary history, theology and practice at present concealed by the Dutch language to be translated and made available in English. Failing such imagination, it may be hoped that some young scholar will dedicate himself to learning Dutch and will then write in English a definitive study of the remarkable contribution made by Dutch missionaries to the modern missionary movement. Needless to say, until the curse of Babel is lifted, there are other possibilities as well!

North Americans, if they read what I have written, will be tempted to dismiss it as very insular. My hope is that some such will be provoked into a similar study of North American missions. There are not a few aspects of North American missionary outreach which are unique and which call for extensive research. It would, for instance, be valuable to have among other studies one which dealt with that peculiarly American phenomenon of the 'family' mission, or the mission sponsored by a single congregation. Again it may be asked, What has it meant for the history of the United States and of her impact on the world that so significant a part has been played in her 'foreign service' by missionaries or by the children of missionary families? 'Spreading the American way of life' and 'carrying the white man's burden', the zeal of Uncle Sam and the pugnacity of John Bull have been curiously parallel in their impact upon modern history, and not least so when their representatives were primarily concerned with spreading the Gospel.

The missionary movement in modern times is waiting for historians who will take seriously its ambiguity without denying its spiritual significance.

I

CHRISTIANITY, COMMERCE AND IMPERIALISM
1729-1834

In 1729 John Wesley returned to Oxford and assumed the leadership of that little company of 'Methodists' already brought together by his brother Charles. Very shortly before, there had been published William Law's devotional classic *A Serious Call to a Devout and Holy Life* which was so greatly to influence John Wesley himself, and the religious life of the century at least as far as 'serious' persons were concerned.

On July 31st, 1834, eight hundred thousand slaves became free. It was one of the greatest events in the history of mankind. And a less dramatic event almost coincided with this act of of liberation. The late Professor Norman Sykes in his book, *Church and State in England in the Eighteenth Century*, has stated that

In consequence of the legislation following upon the report of the Ecclesiastical Commissioners in 1835, the Church of England suffered a second reformation, more thoroughgoing in its financial and administrative purgation than that guided by the hand of the Tudor monarchs.[1]

Those who have read William Law's *Serious Call* will not consider it wholly whimsical to see in the reforms which followed 1835 an attempt to apply to the administrative structure

[1] Norman Sykes, *op. cit.* (Cambridge University Press, 1934) p. 410.

B

of the Church of England the principles which Law proposed for the governance of the individual life. Nevertheless the opening and closing dates which I have chosen are meant to be treated as symbols rather than as indicating any precise limits in time.

It would be easy, and in another context profitable, to show how, during this period and even more in the nineteenth century, Christianity was closely interwoven with both Commerce and Imperialism, infusing into both an element never easily digested, but never wholly absent, and in the sequel enormously complicating the task of historical analysis, while providing not a few of the problems confronting the Christian mission in the world today. The conjunction of these three words, Christianity, Commerce and Imperialism, is here, however, concerned to indicate the fact that the Christianity of the eighteenth and early nineteenth century had as its particular *context* an economic revolution and a remarkable development in the understanding of the meaning of Empire. There is a closer relationship between the three than is commonly appreciated. Of this, at least, we may be certain, that we shall never understand the missionary movement in modern history without some real grasp of its historical context. Indeed, there are not a few contemporary problems in international politics which can best be understood by a true understanding of the missionary movement.

A Time of Exploration

The century which was to see John Wesley and many others exploring the world of religious experience and mapping in a new way the highlands of Christian perfection, was a century which can fairly be described as an age of curiosity. In England the spirit of enquiry, which had taken formal shape in the incorporation by Charter of the Royal Society in 1662 and so provided a forum for a galaxy of men of genius, heralded in the eighteenth century the wider European scientific exploration in which Lavoisier, de Buffon, the Montgolfiers were worthy to be linked with our own Newton, Flamsteed, Boyle and Halley. As one writer has said,

Illumined by the torch of their inspiration and experiments, it (the eighteenth century) was destined to discover and to tame the hidden power of nature. Untold conquests in the material world: a whole universe waiting to be explored: the universal interdependence of all created things: the minute scrutiny of starry spheres and heavenly firmaments: the foundation and basic laws of the whole of modern chemistry! Eighteenth century: Century of Reason: a victorious and triumphant century indeed![2]

But every whit as important as the work of these great thinkers and explorers was that of those who put their knowledge to the test of practical achievement in the economic field. The eighteenth century saw a phenomenal advance in technical skill and equipment. In England there was the harnessing of the water-power of the Pennine springs which gave to Yorkshire and Lancashire their first power mills for the production of cotton and woollen goods. Hargreaves, Arkwright and Crompton laid the foundations of Britain's export trade in textiles. The foundations of one of Britain's best dollar earners today, the export of pottery, were laid by Ralph Wood at Burslem in 1750, while science and art were married by the great Josiah Wedgwood. But for long term significance all of them were perhaps eclipsed by the work of James Watt in perfecting the earlier invention of the steam engine, which more than any other single discovery created the modern world.

Yet we do well to remember the phrase already quoted that the eighteenth century not only recognized 'a whole universe

[2] Maximin Piette, *John Wesley in the Evolution of Protestantism* (Sheed and Ward, 1937), p. 98.

waiting to be explored' but also became aware of 'the universal interdependence of all created things'. This universal interdependence, for good and for evil, must be understood as being true of the religious life of man as of his economic and political activities. They all belong together. The aphorism of John Brown, 'Man does not live by bread alone, but he cannot live without it', is one which we dare never forget if we are to see our Christian mission in perspective.

It would, for instance, be salutary if painful reading, for all who think of the campaigns for the ending of the slave trade, and the emancipation of the slaves, as being one of the few instances in any national history of an act of pure political benevolence, to read a book recently published in England, *Capitalism and Slavery*, by Eric Williams. Since first writing it he has become the Prime Minister of Trinidad. Not all his strictures are fair, some indeed are as unjust as they are untrue. But he certainly establishes the inescapable interdependence of this campaign for abolition with economic developments which assisted the campaign. Sir Denis Brogan, who writes an Introduction, says:

Had the 'West India interest' been as economically powerful at the beginning of the nineteenth century as it was in the middle of the eighteenth, the philanthropists, the Evangelicals, might have agitated and petitioned in vain.[3]

It is possible that Professor Brogan underestimates the moral factors in history, and that Dr Williams misunderstands them. But we do well to take their caution seriously. What any reader of Dr Williams' book must acknowledge is that he has provided adequate documentation for the statement that 'the profits obtained from the slave trade "provided one of the main streams of that accumulation of capital in England which

[3] Eric Williams, *op. cit.* (André Deutsch, 1964), p. vii.

financed the industrial revolution".'[4] James Watt and the development of the steam engine is a case in point. Williams writes:

> It was the capital accumulated from the West Indian trade that financed James Watt and the steam engine. Boulton and Watt received advances from Lowe, Williams and Jennings— later the Williams Deacon's Bank. Watt had some anxious moments in 1778 during the American Revolution when the West Indian fleet was threatened with capture by the French. 'Even in this emergency', wrote Boulton to him hopefully, 'Lowe, Vere and Company may yet be saved, if ye West Indian fleet arrives safe from ye French fleet . . . as many of their securities depend on it'.[5]

By the way, the Williams Deacon's Bank is still the banker of one of our great missionary societies founded in the eighteenth century!

But the eighteenth century explorers opened up new worlds in other ways also. The discoveries of Captain Cook not only provided a great store of new information about the Pacific, but brought a new continent into men's ken. The publication of Captain Cook's *Voyages* captured the imagination of a young cobbler, born at Paulerspury on August 17th, 1761, who was baptized William, with the surname Carey. It is typical of this century of curiosity and exploration that William Carey's book, which can fairly claim to have ushered in the missionary movement in modern history, was entitled *An Enquiry into the Obligations of Christians to use Means for the conversion of the Heathens*. A boy who was so fascinated with the *Life of Columbus* that his schoolmaster nicknamed him after the

---

[4] Eric Williams, *op. cit.*, p. 52. A more recent writer, I. R. Sinai in his book *The Challenge of Modernization—The West's impact on the Non-Western World* (Chatto and Windus, 1964), pp. 49-50, would certainly query the main argument of Dr Williams. He argues that the agricultural revolution marked by enclosures and the breakthrough in technique associated with the steam-engine, together with the surplus wealth extracted from the exploitation of the working classes, provided the main source for the accumulation of capital.

[5] Eric Williams, *op. cit.*, pp. 102-3.

great explorer could not fail to respond to the thrill of reading
the adventures of Captain Cook. It was these great explorers
as well as his New Testament which led him to open his
Enquiry with the words

> Our Lord Jesus Christ, a little before his departure, commis-
> sioned his apostles to *Go* and *teach all nations*; or, as another
> evangelist expresses it, *Go into all the World, and preach the
> Gospel to every creature.* This commission was as extensive as
> possible, and laid them under obligation to disperse themselves
> into every country of the habitable globe, and preach to all the
> inhabitants without exception or limitation.[6]

It was the eighteenth century Carey who, more than any other
man, gave to the modern missionary movement its geographical perspective. And it was Columbus and Captain Cook as
well as St Matthew and St Mark who provided the perspective.
All his contemporaries knew St Matthew's Gospel and St
Mark's Gospel. It was William Carey who saw the 'interdependence' of the Gospels *and* the voyages of Captain Cook *and*
the obligations of the missionary enterprise, and who not only
saw but insisted upon the relevance of this interdependence
for Christian practice.

It would be an interesting subject for research to discover
the relationship between that enlargement of men's horizons
which followed upon the discoveries of Captain Cook, and
the economic revolution which changed the old colonial
system with its Mercantilist philosophy into the practice of
Free Trade.

Eric Williams, in the book already referred to, has an interesting comment when he says that Mercantilism, 'the economic philosophy of the age, had no room for the open door, and
colonial trade was a rigid monopoly of the home country.'[7]
But Captain Cook opened a large number of new doors, too

[6] William Carey, *op. cit.* (Hodder and Stoughton, 1891).
[7] Eric Williams, *op. cit.*, p.55.

many indeed for the old colonial system of monopoly to enter. Spain and Portugal had once tried the policy of monopoly, and the British adventurers had refused to accept it. The successors of those adventurers were to be no more successful in resisting the logic of new discoveries. Eric Williams is most surely true when he claims that 'the attack on the West Indians was more than attack on slavery. It was an attack on monopoly.' He adds, for good measure towards our understanding of interdependence: 'Their opponents were not only the humanitarians but the capitalists.'[8]

The great prophet of economic change, however, was Adam Smith. And once again we have a book with a characteristically eighteenth century title—*An Inquiry into the Nature and Causes of the Wealth of Nations*. In this book Adam Smith called in question the whole Mercantilist economic philosophy which saw the value of colonies as wholly determined by their complete dependence upon the interests of the mother country. What Carey's *Enquiry* did for the consciously Christian mind, this Adam Smith's *Inquiry* did for economists and business men who were slowly becoming aware of the export potentialities of the industrial revolution. Both 'enquiries' were an immense liberation of the human mind, however incomplete that liberation has proved to be. Both enquiries saw this as one world. Each in its own way was an intimation of a goal towards which we still are only painfully making our way, though it may perhaps be claimed with some justice that Carey's logic has been pursued with greater consistency than has that of Adam Smith.

Here may be quoted an interesting paragraph from an American writer, a student of British colonial practice. Professor Knorr, who is Director of the Centre for International Studies at Princeton University, has recently published a volume entitled *British Colonial Theories 1570-1850*. Packed

[8] Eric Williams, *op. cit.*, p. 135.

with detailed information from all kinds of obscure sources it does, albeit incidentally, provide ample evidence of the inter-dependence of Christianity, Commerce and Imperialism during the whole period. Writing of the development from a predominantly mercantile age to a predominantly industrial age, which was to make Britain the 'industrial workshop' of the world, he has this interesting comment:

> This gradual transformation of the political, economic, and social organization of Britain was accompanied by important changes in the sphere of ideas, sentiments, and values. The beginnings of Philosophical Radicalism and the strengthening of the Evangelical revival were two manifestations of this change of spirit which were to leave a distinct imprint on British imperial thinking.[9]

I will not, here, comment on that quotation beyond asking that it be noted as part of the infra-structure of the whole argument of this book. It is more important to note that Adam Smith's *Wealth of Nations* was published in 1776, the year when, rejecting Lord North's attempts at reconciliation, the American Colonies finally revolted. It is, indeed, interesting to observe that, in part at least, Adam Smith's argument was a last-minute appeal to sanity in an attempt to persuade the British Government that Mercantilism was a false philosophy, and that there was no need for there to be any separation between Britain and her American colonies. Had his arguments been heeded, this second civil war between Englishmen could have been as happily resolved as was the earlier civil war of the seventeenth century. The economic sequel was to show that Adam Smith was right.

Freedom was in the air. In Christianity men were experimenting in a new freedom, or, if you prefer it, in the original freedom. On the continent the Moravians had formed their community, and there was the beginning of the fertilization

---

[9] Klaus Knorr, *op. cit.* (Frank Cass and Co., Ltd., 1963), p. 155.

of Lutheranism by the Pietist movement. Likewise on the continent Jansenism produced the Old Catholics.

Within the Roman Catholic Church there was its own particular form of 'enthusiasm' which found liturgical expression in the devotion to the Sacred Heart of Jesus, and an evangelistic expression in the Redemptorist Order founded by St Alfonzo Liguori. In England the experiments towards a new liberation are associated with the Wesleys, Whitefield, and the Evangelical revival, which on the other side of the Atlantic had the prophetic leadership of Jonathan Edwards. However diverse these religious experiments may have been, they were all expressions of that new urge towards the freedom of the human spirit which in economic terms betokened the end of an age of monopoly, and in the political field saw the declaration of the 'rights of Man' expressed first in the American and then in the French Revolution.

We should not pretend that, at the time, there was any recognition of the 'interdependence' of all these manifestations of revolt against conformity. But with hindsight at our disposal we can see that they did all represent a common movement in the spirit of man. Nor must we lightly determine at what points in this common urge we draw the line between what was of the Spirit of God and what was not. We are still sadly lacking in any comprehensive theology of the divine lordship over history.

It cannot be accidental that a scholar like Professor Knorr, who, to judge by his book is no exaggerated partisan of the Christian religion, should make the following summary of the humanitarian movement of the eighteenth century:

The new humanitarian spirit sprang from two different sources. First, it originated in eighteenth-century enlightenment, in the intellectual temper that produced the French Revolution. Its spirit of egalitarianism and brotherhood and its belief in human perfectibility found expression in a novel code of humanitarian ethics. Secondly, it issued in the Evangelical movement which had been growing steadily since its inception by the early Methodists. Thus, in respect of many objects of reform, there was an alliance, though not in spirit and motivation, between the Evangelicals and the Benthamites.[10]

The Idea of Trusteeship

Another element in the historical background must be understood, for it was destined to play a very great part in the story of nineteenth century imperialism, and its influence is with us still: the concept of trusteeship, more particularly as that is understood in political terms.

No one who appreciates the tenacious grip which Mercantilist thinking had on the generality of business men and politicians during the greater part of the eighteenth century will imagine that the idea of trusteeship made its way easily. As early as 1732, indeed, General Oglethorpe told the House of Commons:

In all cases that come before this House, where there seems to be a clashing of interests between one set of people and another, we ought to have no regard to the particular interest of any country or any set of people; the good of the whole is what we ought only to have under our consideration: our colonies are all a part of our own dominions: the people in every one of them are our people, and we ought to show an equal respect to all.

But his was a voice crying in a wilderness of scepticism if not of downright hostility. Indeed we have hardly caught up with that vision yet. Nevertheless General Oglethorpe introduced an idea which was destined slowly but surely to win its way. Thirty-six years later Thomas Pownall in a book entitled *The Administration of the Colonies* developed the vision a little further. He dreamed of a British Empire in which

[10] Klaus Knorr, *op. cit.*, p. 376.

Great Britain may be no more considered as the Kingdom of this Isle only, with many appendages of provinces, colonies, settlements, and other extraneous parts, but as a Grand Marine Dominion consisting of our Possessions in the Atlantic and in America United into One Empire.

He added:

The centre of power instead of remaining fixed as it now is in Great Britain, will, as the magnitude of the power and interest of the Colonies increases, be drawn out from the island. . . .[11]

History has fulfilled that dream in an unexpected way. But our fumbling attempts at an Atlantic Alliance and the practical transfer of the 'centre of power' to Washington shows that Pownall had foresight. And he was by no means the only man to think thus widely in that century.[12]

From another point of view altogether English dissenters tended to view the colonies after the same fashion. Yet all of these remained minority opinions. It was the combination of these minority opinions, together with the shock of the loss of the American colonies, and fears generated by the ideas of the French Revolution, combined with the increasingly widespread diffusion of humanitarian principles and the force of the Evangelical Revival—a queerly assorted combination—which compelled the politicians to pay increasing attention to the idea of 'trusteeship'. But it can, I think, be plausibly maintained that the driving force which brought the realization of the ideal of trusteeship as far as it had reached by the middle of the twentieth century, was an increasingly robust Christian conscience and sense of responsibility.

[11] Thomas Pownall, *The Administration of the Colonies* (J. Walter, London, 1768), pp. 9-10, 37.

[12] See Adam Smith, *Wealth of Nations*, Book IV, Chapter 7, Part 3, and Arthur Young, *Political Essays concerning the Present State of the British Empire* (W. Strahan and T. Cadell, London, 1772), esp. Essay V, 'The Present State of the British Colonies'.

Let it be stressed again that the progress towards the ideal of trusteeship for dependent peoples was slow and uneven. Always there have been strong groups of people, often in influential positions, who have seen Empire solely in terms of a good business proposition or as conducive to prestige. Yet part of the intention of this book is to underline the abiding importance of responsible minorities and to afford a reminder, as much needed today as ever, that God is not always on the side of the big battalions.

Professor Knorr, in his researches, has amassed sufficient evidence to justify one of his conclusions, which is that

> The development of the notion of Britain's supreme mission to civilize the world by means of her far-flung Empire began with the downfall of the first Empire. . . . It would be wrong to assume that this new phenomenon owed its existence to the crafty propagandist effort of an imperial class that observed the emergence of social and economic forces with inherent anti-imperial tendencies. The evolution of this new sentiment was intimately connected with the general development of a powerful humanitarian current in the spiritual life of the English people. From its very beginning the manifestations of this new imperial sentimentalism revealed the existence of genuine feeling of concern for the lot of the coloured peoples and a deep sense of duty.[13]

'Genuine feeling of concern for the lot of the coloured peoples and a deep sense of duty'—let us mark those words, and give them their very fullest value. They are a key to much in the history of the missionary movement. Professor Knorr is right in going on to say that as touching our national 'imperial sentimentalism' there was all too much insincerity and arrogance. All too much humbug has characterized much British thinking, writing and speaking about the 'white man's burden', about our dependent peoples as being wards and ourselves as trustees. Resentment against this attitude goes far to explain

[13] Klaus Knorr, *op. cit.*, pp. 246-247.

many contemporary attitudes on the part of Asians and Africans today. Let us make the fullest allowance for our irritating national habit of expressing our invariable sense of superiority under the disguise of high moral seriousness. But do not let us forget what Professor Knorr speaks of as 'a genuine feeling of concern for the lot of the coloured peoples and a deep sense of duty'.

In 1823 the Church Missionary Society sent twelve missionaries to Sierra Leone. Within eighteen months ten of them were dead from fever. In the language of an earlier day we read these words of how the news was received in England:

> The Committee were for the moment crushed by all this overwhelming sorrow. They gazed in one another's faces across the table; they knelt together at the footstool of the Divine Mercy; and the tradition is that one leading lay member, on the day that the news came of the several deaths, rose and said in a tone of deep feeling and resolve, 'We must *not* abandon West Africa'.[14]

The Society did not abandon West Africa. And it is on record that whenever one man fell there was always another who volunteered to take his place. That is worth remembering in our rather easy-going generation. 'A genuine sense of concern' and 'a deep sense of duty' have not been mere words in the missionary movement in modern history.

It is that record which has to be borne in mind when we listen to the florid periods which occur in the speeches of nineteenth century politicians. We may smile at the ebullience of Huskisson addressing the House of Commons in 1828 and saying in regard to Canada:

> We have everywhere displayed marks of paternal government, and planted improvement, not only on our colonies there, but wherever our Empire is acknowledged . . . Sir, England is the

[14] Eugene Stock, *History of the Church Missionary Society* (C.M.S., 1899), vol. i, p. 170.

parent of many flourishing colonies . . . In every quarter of the globe we have planted the seeds of freedom, civilization and Christianity.[15]

But while we smile, do not let us forget those graves in Sierra Leone.

The Evangelical Revival

We may turn to look more carefully at eighteenth century religion in this country.

If we are to understand the Evangelical Revival and the form it took in the eighteenth century, and something of the permanent impress which its genesis in that century has laid on all subsequent generations, we must pay some attention to two strands of influence which are clues to much that followed.

The first strand consists in the multiplication of religious societies which arose in England, for the most part after the revolution of 1688. By the beginning of Queen Anne's reign there were, for instance, one hundred such societies in London alone. The primary end of these societies was the spiritual renovation of the country. Their members met together regularly for prayer and Bible Study, but their intention was always to see what steps could be taken to put their concerns into practical effect. It was charactertistic of them that each member made it his object to preach by example and to live in strict loyalty to the Established Church, attending its services and receiving its sacraments. It is of some interest to remember that the Society for the Reformation of Manners which came into existence in 1692 was followed six years later by the Society for Promoting Christian Knowledge. And in 1801 there was founded the Society for the Propagation of the Gospel in Foreign Parts. Those two venerable missionary societies, at the very beginning of the period we are studying,

[15] Robert Walsh, *Select Speeches of William Windham and William Huskisson* (Philadelphia, 1845), pp. 543f., quoted by Klaus Knorr, *op. cit.*, p. 366.

sprang out of the ferment which was producing these many religious societies.

The enduring importance of this particular religious ferment lies in the fact that it took the form of a voluntary association for religious purposes of men who had a deep concern for a vital and practical religion. Furthermore it is important to note that the principle of order was strongly enshrined in these societies. In intention there was no desire to promote schism, but rather the very reverse, to stimulate within the Established Church the spirit of true religion.

Many of these societies were short-lived, though two of the originals are with us still. Some of these early societies allowed misguided zeal for the reformation of manners to bring their whole purpose into disrepute. But the idea which they represented bore fruit. And in the Holy Club at Oxford, and subsequently in the organization of Methodism, we can see clearly how John Wesley himself was only carrying into effect an idea which was already familiar to serious-minded persons. The originality of Wesley is to be found neither in his organization nor in the doctrines which he promulgated, so much as in the dynamic power with which he galvanized the multitudes, so that what had been small coteries of earnest Christians became a great movement of opinion both inside and outside the Established Church, and, indeed, outside the Churches altogether.

What is very important for us to note is that these societies by their very nature safeguarded religion from becoming quietist and individualist. Maximin Piette records the words of that serious man who said to John Wesley:

Sir, you wish to serve God and go to heaven? Remember that you cannot serve him alone. You must therefore find companions or make them; the Bible knows nothing of solitary religion.

Shortly after that encounter John Wesley was recalled to

Lincoln College, Oxford, to discharge his duties as a junior Fellow. We know that on his return he joined the little company of men already gathered together by his brother Charles. As Piette remarks:

> Apostolic zeal is shortly to flood the soul of this young man, who had hitherto spent his energies almost exclusively in conquering himself. The Wesleyan Movement is about to commence: from being individual he is to become social.[16]

Nor in making that quotation ought we to underestimate the spiritual importance of the fact that as a junior Fellow of his college John Wesley had certain social responsibilities, among them the charge of eleven students, not to mention the care of a neighbouring parish.

The second strand in the religious preparation for the Evangelical Revival was the influence of William Law and more particularly of his book *A Serious Call to a Devout and Holy Life*.

No one can read this book and fail to see the profound influence that it had on John Wesley. Later in life his own temperament led him away from William Law's mysticism. But the whole emphasis of this book on a disciplined life, a discipline to be revealed in its methodical application to everyday living as well as to private devotion, was dramatically illustrated in Wesley's own life and teaching. No reader will forget the way in which Law writes of the intention to please God in all one's actions and then illustrates it by saying:

> Let a tradesman but have this intention, and it will make him a saint in his shop: his every-day business will be a course of wise and reasonable actions made holy to God, by being done in obedience to His will and pleasure ... He will consider what arts, or methods, or application can make worldly business most acceptable to God, and make a life of trade a life of holiness, devotion and piety.[17]

[16] Maximin Piette, *op. cit.*, pp. 271-272.
[17] William Law, *op. cit.* (Everyman ed., Dent, 1940), p. 14.

In that very illustration we can see the source of an inspiration which through Wesley's influence has transformed the living of countless men and women, from small shopkeepers and typists to great merchants and leaders of industry. Here was the fertile source which has irrigated with Christian insights whole ranges of our national life for two hundred years. Here was the eighteenth century premonition of that 'Holy Worldliness' which we are coming to recognize as so indispensable for the spiritual renewal of our national life today.

It is in this context that we are to understand the central heart of Wesley's doctrine of 'Christian Perfection'. This was no otherworldly ideal. William Law had taught him to see it as something which could be experienced by a tradesman behind his counter, or a miner at the coal-face, *and* no less possible for a society-darling or a member of the Cabinet. And somewhere in the middle of such a variegated company would be found a Dr Johnson who could testify that Law's *Serious Call* was the first occasion of his 'thinking in earnest of religion after he became capable of rational enquiry'. I like that sober eighteenth-century assessment.

These two strands of influence on John Wesley became of far-reaching importance in the story of the Evangelical Revival, and contributed their meed to the later religious movements of the nineteenth century. Law's *Serious Call* profoundly influenced Charles Simeon and many another Evangelical leader within the Church of England as the eighteenth century made way for the nineteenth. As important was the continuing influence of the idea of voluntary religious societies held together by a common aim and a strong interior discipline. There is something wholly one-sided and inaccurate in the popular picture of Evangelical religion as being one of almost unbridled individualism. The disciplined fellowship of religious societies is the real clue to Evangelical religion. A careful modern historian, the late Dr M. G. Jones, insisted on

c

the importance of the specifically religious element in the humanitarianism of the eighteenth century. She wrote of how 'the religious revivals, by stressing the sense of individual responsibility, changed a trickle of private and semi-private benevolence into a spate of organized philanthropy.'[18] 'Individual responsibility' and 'organized philanthropy'—those two phrases must be held together, as, in practice, they belonged together. They are the two expressions of eighteenth century religion, as it was transformed by the Evangelical Revival, which most profoundly influenced the subsequent life of Britain, and of a large part of mankind.

Believing that as I do, I am the more ready to face frankly the fact that the missionary movement as it emerged in modern history was no pure stream flowing in crystal purity from the throne of God. From the start it was a strange admixture of the human and the divine. Because in the next chapter we will be concerned with missionary motives I am the more ready to close this one with the somewhat mordant comment of Professor Knorr. It is an unsympathetic summary of our findings so far. He writes:

This new humanitarian outlook in imperial thinking was not without opposition, but it is no exaggeration to say that as a matter of principle and sentiment it was accepted by the British nation and permeated its councils. The idea of Trusteeship over coloured peoples obviously was a powerful phenomenon in the thirties and forties of the nineteenth century. Of course, missionary imperialism of any kind, whether it embraces the spread of an entire culture or only part of it, may constitute the conferring of benefits on peoples of a so-called inferior culture or religion from the point of view of the missionary nation. But . . . it may turn out to be 'a greater trial to subject races than a more primitive and not self-conscious form of exploitation'. For missionary imperialism does not even permit such peoples to live

[18] M. G. Jones, *Hannah More 1745-1833* (Cambridge University Press, 1952), p. 81.

their own lives, to worship their Gods, and to preserve their institutions and customs.[19]

That is a fashionable modern criticism. It will be our task in subsequent chapters to consider the measure of truth which it contains, and to judge whether in fact the religious initiatives of the eighteenth century have in the end run out into the spiritual desert envisaged by Professor Knorr's dictum. And we must also take very seriously that formidable conjunction of words—'missionary imperialism'. Our study, I hope, will throw some new light on both words. It should also provide us with some material for a critique of the current fashion of joining the two words and thereby finding a valid ground for the final condemnation of the missionary movement in modern history.

[19] Klaus Knorr, *op. cit.*, p. 388.

2

MISSIONARY MOTIVES
1789-1859

THE storming of the Bastille on July 14th, 1789, the date commonly accepted for the beginning of the French Revolution, will at first sight seem strangely unrelated to that moving of the Spirit which ushered in the most dramatic period of expansion in the history of the Christian Church. Yet the fervour which drove the disciples of Rousseau to attempt the political realization of his theories is in some respects strangely akin to that which animated the men who responded to the challenge of religious renewal thrown down by the Wesleys. Both in their respective ways were reactions to any theoretical faith, secular or religious, which refused to work itself out in life.

1789, then, may well serve as a symbol for the beginning of that release of revolutionary energy which has been the dynamic lying behind all political change from that day to this. In the same year the Eclectic Society in London, a group of as yet unknown and undistinguished clergy and laity, took for their subject of discussion on February 16th the question 'What is the best method of propagating the Gospel in the East Indies?' That was no casual choice of a subject by a debating society. A chaplain of the East India Company in Bengal, David Brown, and a number of the Company's officials, had forwarded to England 'A proposal for establishing a Protestant Mission in Bengal and Behar'. Nor was it an isolated phenomenon. The same group had already in 1786 been discussing a similar project in regard to Australia.

Meanwhile, in other circles besides the Church of England members of the Eclectic Society, imaginations were being stirred. In the Church Book of Olney there was already an entry for the year 1786 about the call to the ministry of one William Carey which runs: 'Sent out by the Church to preach the Gospel wherever God in His providence might call him.'[1] The 'wherever' in that sentence, as we saw in the last chapter, was not unrelated to Carey's reading of the *Voyages* of Captain Cook which began to be published in 1784. In 1789 Carey became a Baptist minister in Leicester, and never ceased to press the subject of Missions upon the attention of his fellow-ministers. 1789 also saw the first of William Wilberforce's great Parliamentary speeches on the subject of slavery.

What is more, practice was trying to keep pace with theory among these 'enthusiasts' in England as surely as among the 'enthusiasts' in France. In 1787 the Colony of Sierra Leone was established with the explicit purpose of doing something to alleviate the lot of negro beggars in England, and of freed slaves who, after Lord Mansfield's judgment in 1772, were able to claim the protection of the English Courts of Law. The early vicissitudes of the new Colony of Sierra Leone may have been the result of ignorance and faulty planning. What cannot be disputed is the seriousness of the intention to match theory with practice.

We may, then, fairly claim 1789 as a year to which we can look back as to a time when ideas, religious no less than political, which had been slowly smouldering, ignited to start a chain reaction of explosions whose effects are with us still. No doubt the changes in men's economic thinking and in

---

[1] From the Introduction to the 1891 edition of *An Enquiry into the Obligations of Christians to use Means for the Conversion of the Heathens*, by William Carey (Hodder & Stoughton, 1891), p. xiii.

their political thinking were far more closely related to the growth of humanitarian thought and religious renewal than was always perceived at the time. From our perspective nearly two centuries later we can see this relationship clearly. What I have attempted here, briefly, to indicate is that, integral to the whole ferment of ideas associated with the last quarter of the eighteenth century, was the beginning of a revolution in Christian thinking which was to lead to a revolution in Christian action. 'The world is my parish' said John Wesley, thereby, in more senses than one, plotting out the range of the Christian mission.

A Revival and its Results

The year 1859 is chosen as the closing date of our present subject, for one simple reason. In that year there occurred first in Northern Ireland a movement of religious revival which is still but little noticed even by church historians. The revival soon spread in Britain, as it had already started in America. I would, myself, hazard the judgment that there is little hope of understanding the story of the missionary movement of the Christian Church, whether in ancient or in modern times, if we fail to give full value to the spiritual influences which have moved Christians of the rank and file. Great leaders, whose names are known to everyone, are great leaders precisely because they have great numbers of people to lead. And the led are not only moved by the great leader. As Christians we must surely prefer to say that the many are primarily moved by the Holy Spirit of God. The great human leader gives form and direction to the manifold responses of individuals who have first been moved by the Holy Spirit. That is an important element in the Christian understanding of history. Later in this chapter we shall find some evidence of this for the period under consideration. But the principle stands for all ages. And it is perhaps the more important that the principle be grasped when a movement, such as the 1859 revival, does not find a focus in some leading personality. The 1859 revival in Britain and the comparable movement in the United States had no John Wesley, no Whitefield. But they profoundly influenced the future of the missionary enterprise at those subordinate levels where ordinary men and women make their individual decision about loyalty to God and obedience to his will.

The 1859 revival was directly responsible for two developments which were to be of far more than temporary significance. The first was the inauguration of the annual 'Universal Week of Prayer', by which Christians of many allegiances have since that date been brought together once a year to pray for the spiritual renewal of the Church and to rededicate themselves to its mission. This movement of united prayer and of prayer for unity has developed in many directions since 1859. What can hardly be questioned has been its importance for the Christian Church throughout the world during the past century, more particularly at the level of the rank and file of the Church.[2]

The second development which followed from the 1859 revival was the holding in Liverpool in 1860 of the first United Missionary Conference. A small affair as touching numbers, it was the prelude to much larger conferences in London in 1878 and 1888. It was the precursor of the great Conference at Edinburgh in 1910, and therefore in a real sense one progenitor of the Ecumenical Movement of today.[3]

Having attempted a definition, under two symbolic dates, of the limits of our subject, let me indicate one serious diffi-

[2] Prayer had been central to the activities of the 'World's Evangelical Alliance' since its foundation in 1846. But it was the stimulus of the 1859 Revival which began to give it a 'universal' character.
[3] A careful and scholarly account of the Revival and its subsequent influences is to be found in J. Edwin Orr, *The Second Evangelical Awakening in Britain* (Marshall, Morgan and Scott, 1949).

culty which confronts anyone who today tries to understand
the missionary motives which influenced Christians in the
period under review. Our main difficulty is one of language.
It is, let us be frank, a somewhat tedious business to read
through the sermons of the period. It is not that their matter
was inadequate. As touching matter many of them are in-
finitely more adequate as declarations of the whole counsel of
God than are all too many contemporary exhortations which
in their desire to be 'with it' are generally without any clear
connection with the Word of God. What, however, is exhaust-
ing about the sermons of that period is their prolixity of style,
and the massive scale of their argumentation. In all this, proportion can be gained if we remember their contemporaries;
if we read again the great Johnsonian periods, and the rhetoric
of Burke and Pitt. In those days there was time to listen to
long speeches and long sermons, and the speaker, be he in
Parliament or pulpit, was expected to unfold his theme at
generous length.

There is another difference between that age and ours which
makes for dull reading. Those who spoke in public in that
age, if they spoke on matters of moment, tended towards a
style of magisterial *gravitas* which is very remote from our
mood today.

All this must be taken into consideration in our approach
to the minds of the men we shall be considering. Historical-
mindedness demands that we try to get behind the forms of
speech to the speaker, and to remember that the speaker was
a man speaking within the context of his age and not ours,
with the visions and limitations, the hopes and fears, which
marked his time and which are different from ours.

There is on the files of the War Office, so Sir Winston
Churchill assured us, a memorandum by a General officer of
long experience in the Napoleonic wars, urging the desirability of arming British regiments with the long-bow instead

of with muskets. There was cogency in his argument, for the rapidity, range of fire, and lethal effect of the long-bowmen at Crécy were unsurpassed until the introduction of the modern rifle.[4]

That unlikely illustration is given merely to indicate that in thinking about the eighteenth and early nineteenth centuries we will find ourselves in a world of assumptions very remote from our own. We must divest ourselves of many of our habits of thought and the ways in which our thinking is expressed, if we are to enter with sympathy into the minds of the men of our period whose missionary motives were, under God, the secret of the modern expansion of the Christian faith in all parts of the world. If we would understand the significance of the fact that there is a Church today in China and Japan; if we seek for the explanation as to why Indian politicians, when they exhort their fellow-countrymen to self-sacrifice and public service, commonly do so by recommending 'a missionary spirit'; if we would discover the inner springs of much of the fervour of African nationalism; in all these respects and many others we must for our understanding go back to the eighteenth century. There we must study even those dull sermons and equally dull records of meetings of serious-minded men like those who constituted the Eclectic and similar societies, whose thoughts, so ponderously expressed, yet served to galvanize so many of their hearers into new spiritual life and encourage them to undertake such incredible spiritual adventures.

Cultural Imperialism or Christian Obedience?

After that, perhaps, overlong exordium we may launch out into the deeps of our subject. I quote again from Professor Knorr's *British Colonial Theories, 1570-1850*. The extract

[4] Winston S. Churchill, *A History of the English Speaking Peoples* (Cassell, 1962), vol. i, p. 236.

given at the end of the last chapter faithfully mirrors a good deal of current opinion on the missionary movement. More briefly, and more pungently, in another place he states that the missionary movement from approximately 1789 until the 1830s was 'in essence . . . an aggressive cultural imperialism, propaganda for the spread of European ideas and ideals over the face of the globe.'[5]

It would not be at all difficult to produce evidence which would support that judgment, provided we observe two caveats. First, in relation to the world outside Europe the period in question was not self-critical. The infinite superiority, from every point of view, of Western society over the heathen world was axiomatic. When the *Missionary Register* was started in 1813 its editor, after referring to the paganism of the earliest centuries of our history, addressed his readers thus:

> You now are a favoured nation: your light is come: the glory of the Lord is risen upon you: all these heathen rites have ceased: the blood of the victims no longer flows: an established Christian Church lifts its venerable head: the pure Gospel is preached: ministers of the sanctuary, as heralds of salvation, proclaim mercy throughout the land—while civil and religious liberty has grown up under the benign influence of the Gospel, that sacred tree, the leaves of which are for the healing of the nations.[6]

There is no hint in that piece of rhetoric to suggest that the country labourer and the town artisan of the period were in abject poverty: that in that very year 1813 Parliament repealed the Elizabethan statutes which gave magistrates power to enforce a minimum wage, thus leaving the working man unprotected as to wages, hours and factory conditions: that repressive legislation prompted by anti-Jacobin fears was still

[5] Klaus Knorr, *op. cit.*, p. 381.

[6] *The Missionary Register for the year 1813, containing an abstract of the Proceedings of the Principal Missionary and Bible Societies throughout the world* (L. B. Seeley, London), vol. i, p. 8.

in force: that religious liberty outside the Established Church was still restricted.

By and large it was certainly not a self-critical generation and some of its blind-spots were remarkable as judged by our own short-sightedness. But that is not the whole story. The second caveat to be entered before accepting Professor Knorr's devastating judgment is his use of the word 'essence'. Was the 'essence' of the missionary movement really 'cultural imperialism'? More is at stake in arriving at a right answer to that question than providing an answer to Professor Knorr. We must be prepared to consider very carefully the interaction of religion and culture, their quite inescapable association at all times and in all circumstances, and then to judge what this has to say about both religion and culture. In subsequent chapters we may find that Professor Knorr is a little cavalier in his judgment, as are the many who accept his assumptions.

That very quotation from the *Missionary Register* continues with the writer apostrophizing his readers in the following terms:

Christians! to whom under God, do you owe all these blessings? You owe them to that man, who was the first Missionary to Great Britain. He came with his Bible and his life in his hand, ready to be offered. He came with the love of God shed abroad in his heart, willing to die for His sake who had died for him; seeking not yours, but you.[7]

In that sequel to his earlier rhetoric the editor of the *Missionary Register* is giving in essence the mission of Columba and Aidan, of Augustine and Boniface, of Raymond Lull and Francis Xavier, of John Eliot and Brainerd, of Schwartz and Carey and Henry Martyn. In this second quotation then is no rhetoric but a simple statement of facts which can be docu-

---

[7] *Ibid.*, p. 28.

mented from the New Testament down until our own day. No doubt the man who was 'ready to be offered' was at one moment a Roman citizen of Jewish birth, at another a celtic prince, a medieval monk, a friar, or a New England minister, or a Baptist cobbler or even a Cambridge graduate, each the product and expression of the culture in which he was born. But the essence of what the man was was that he was 'ready to be offered', that the love of God had been shed abroad in his heart, and that 'he was willing to die for His sake who had died for him.' The story of the missionary movement can record countless missionaries who were resented as bringing with them an alien and uncongenial culture. Not infrequently this led to their suffering violence. Often they were in fact 'offered'. But their own self-offering was not in the name of their culture. It was in the name of 'Him who had died for *them*'. To grasp that fact is to grasp the essence of the missionary movement. It is to discover one, and not the least important, of the many clues to the course of events in our contemporary world.

To claim that second quotation from the *Missionary Register* as more significant than the first one, which revealed a singularly un-self-critical attitude to the situation in England at the time, is not to justify that lack of self-criticism. Blindness is always blindness whether in our own or in earlier generations. And because blindness tends to generate *hubris* we know that *nemesis* is never far away, though as Christians we will prefer to think of the divine judgment, in which there is always mercy.

With this general picture of missionary motivation in mind, true as it is for every age, it is possible to approach with more understanding the particular motives which in our period of study moved men and women to offer for missionary work and service. As far as possible I will let the men of that period speak for themselves in their own words. Before doing so, however, I would refer you to that very comprehensive study of our subject by the Dutch writer, Johannes Van Den Berg.[8] This is a most thorough exploration of the evidence. The interest of his argument lies in the variety of motives which he discovers, in their not infrequent concurrence in the same individual, and in the progressive concentration, as the period of his study is reviewed, of one dominant motive, the one which he has chosen for the title of his book.

I believe Dr Van Den Berg's analysis to be accurate. I, therefore propose to list the motives which he discerns as operating to promote the missionary enterprise, and to follow this with evidence from some of the original sources which I have myself explored. His book itself is quite indispensable for the serious student of this subject and this period.

First, in order of treatment, Van Den Berg puts the *utilitarian* motive which, while never primary, yet had its appeal for some. Claudius Buchanan in 1812 cites as the second reason for inculcating our religion the reason that 'it attaches the governed to their governors'.[9] Or again there is John Williams of the London Missionary Society, who, on the eve of sailing for the Pacific in 1817 could say, 'everyone, who is concerned to promote the commercial welfare of his country, is bound to exert himself on behalf of the Missionary Society'. But before passing an adverse judgment on that remark it may be not unfair to set it in the context of a widespread debate throughout the country in which only a little earlier (1811) Samuel Butler, who was later to become Bishop of Lichfield, had written, 'Unless our Government act cautiously, methodistical proselytizers, by their absurd enthusiasm, will bring about the loss of India'. Bad arguments sometimes provoke

---

[8] Johannes Van Den Berg, *Constrained by Jesus' Love: An Inquiry into the Motives of the Missionary Awakening in Great Britain in the Period between 1698 and 1815*, (J. K. Kok, N. V., Kampen, Netherlands, 1956).

[9] Claudius Buchanan, *Memoir of the Expediency of an Ecclesiastical Establishment for British India*, (London, 1812), p. 36.

bad arguments. John Williams was certainly not primarily interested in commerce.

Second, Van Den Berg lists what he calls *humanitarian-cultural* motives. He quotes William Carey, for instance, as saying among much else about the obligations of Christians towards the heathen

Can we hear that they are without the Gospel, without government, without laws, and without arts and sciences; and not exert ourselves to introduce amongst them the sentiments of men and of Christians? Would not the spread of the Gospel be the most effectual means of their civilization? Would not that make them useful members of society?[10]

That was William Carey writing before he went to India. It faithfully reflects that sense of the superiority of eighteenth century English civilization over all other sorts. But it is an argument *ad hominem,* it is not William Carey's real motive. Yet it remains part of the picture and must be included.

Third comes *the ascetic motive.* Van Den Berg gives as his only illustration of this that remarkable missionary saint and one-time scholar of St John's College, Cambridge, Henry Martyn, showing how deeply he had been moved by the asceticism of two of his missionary heroes David Brainerd, missionary to the North American Indians, and Francis Xavier. But I think Van Den Berg could also have quoted John Wesley, and there can be little doubt that William Law's asceticism is never very far in the background of the thinking of many of the first protagonists of Missions during this period.

The *fourth* motive is that of *debt.* To this I will be referring at greater length. A *fifth* motive is described under the heading *romantic.* Professor Knorr goes so far as to say that the missionary 'task, greatly romanticized, carried the gratifying flavour of adventure.'[11] We should not discount this element.

[10] William Carey, *op. cit.,* p. 70.   [11] Klaus Knorr, *op. cit.,* p. 381.

But Van Den Berg has wisdom and truth with him when he writes:

The pioneer of modern British missions, Carey, had read with more than ordinary interest the accounts of the South Sea voyages: they found an echo with him because, no doubt, he had been touched with the romantic spirit which was in the air; partly through them, his eyes were opened to the problems of the wider world. But though without a certain disposition for romance and adventure Carey would perhaps never have become the man whom history honours as a missionary leader of broad vision and admirable courage, it would be quite wrong to see him as a romantic dreamer.[12]

Of Van Den Berg's *sixth* motive, *the theocentric motive,* and seventh, *the motive of love and compassion,* there will be more to say. His *eighth* motive is designated *ecclesiological.* Wherever a very strong denominational emphasis based on some view of Church Order is prevalent, then it is likely that the idea of a *plantatio ecclesiae* will be a powerful motive towards missionary service. This has undoubtedly been in the past, as it still is, a motive of very considerable influence. But it would be a most unfair conclusion to judge this as no more than denominational imperialism. It may degenerate into that. At its heart however is the sincere conviction of those who hold this view, that the very form of the Church is part of the Church's Gospel. During our period, however, from 1789-1859 this motive, if present at all, was present in a curiously Erastian form, as may be judged from the debates in Parliament over the renewal of the East India Company's Charter in 1813 in which the proposal for the setting up of a Church Establishment in India was successfully introduced.[13]

The *ninth* motive is described as *eschatological.* The evi-

[12] J. Van Den Berg, *op. cit.,* p. 153.
[13] See Ainslee Embree, *Charles Grant and British Rule in India* (Allen and Unwin, 1962).

dence points to a specific, and for our generation, a little considered aspect of eschatological thinking. In so far as this motive is apparent it is concerned almost entirely with the anticipated millennium. There is no awareness either of 'realized eschatology' or, except rarely, of any thought of a judgment bringing history to an end. David Brown, already mentioned as a chaplain of the East India Company, may speak for the majority opinion. Of him Charles Simeon said that his belief 'was strengthened by the signs of the times, that the great purposes of God were about to be accomplished in the conversion of the nations to the faith of Christ.'[14] But this can be capped by that heroic spirit, Henry Martyn:

> While I write, hope and joy shall spring up in my mind. Yes, it shall be, yonder stream of Ganges shall one day roll through tracts adorned with Christian Churches. . . . All things are working together to bring on the day.[15]

Those two passages, and many others, might indeed be taken as evidence of the romantic as much as of the eschatological motive. What is largely absent in our period, in comparison with this note of hopefulness, is that emphasis on the heathen perishing in their blindness, which was to be so powerful a motive in the second half of the nineteenth century.

Van Den Berg's *tenth* motive, which must concern us at greater length, is the motive of *obedience* to Christ's explicit commission.

An Estimate of the Motives

Van Den Berg's analysis, based as it is on voluminous reading, is here presented primarily to underline the wide variety of influence which played on the minds of those who, in this

[14] Charles Simeon, *Memorial Sketches of the Rev. David Brown* (London, 1816), p. 75.

[15] H. Martyn, *Journals and Letters*, ed. S. Wilberforce (London, 1837), vol. ii, p. 272.

period, committed themselves to promoting missions to the heathen. It is important to realize how varied were these motives, and to remember that they were effective in inspiring a steadily growing number of ordinary people. They became an integral part of the devotion of countless simple people, thereby creating a certain spiritual climate which has to be recognized as underlying the whole outlook of the Victorian age. It was a climate which gave to that age its peculiar quality of gravity, high purpose, and sanguine hopefulness, a combination of qualities which we in our more troubled times find it hard to understand.

My own analysis differs in some respects from that of Van Den Berg but I offer it not in contradiction but rather as a complement, adding a few motives which, so it seems to me, he underestimates, and giving to others a different slant. There were other motives to which Van Den Berg does full justice, but which so far have been noticed only in passing.

I begin with the need to make reparation for the Slave Trade. As is well known, Albert Schweitzer has devoted his life to medical work at Lambarene in Gabon with this primary motive. But it was a motive which operated powerfully in the minds of many at the end of the eighteenth century.

Giving his charge to two German missionaries, the first missionaries sent out by the Church Missionary Society, Josiah Pratt on January 31st, 1804, spoke as follows:

The temporal misery of the whole Heathen World has been dreadfully aggravated, by its intercourse with men who bear the name of Christians; but the Western Coast of Africa between the Tropics, and more especially that part between the Line and the Tropic of Cancer, has not only, in common with other heathen countries, received from us our diseases and our vices, but it has even been the chief theatre of the inhuman Slave Trade; and tens of thousands of its children have been annually torn from their dearest connections, to minister to the luxuries of men bearing the Christian name . . . and though Western Africa may

D

justly charge her sufferings from the trade upon all Europe directly or remotely, yet the British nation is now and has long been most deeply criminal. We desire, therefore, while we pray and labour for the removal of this evil, to make Western Africa the best remuneration in our power for its manifold wrongs.[16]

Nine years later the same Josiah Pratt speaking at a public meeting in Bristol said:

A thousand African children may be brought under the Christian care of our missionaries, if your liberality, and that of other friends shall enable us so far to extend our efforts. And let it be considered, sir, that this scene of Christian benevolence is opening on a shore which Britain has deeply injured. From this city, sir, Africa has received many of her wounds.[17]

Josiah Pratt was by far and away the most important publicist for the missionary cause in the first twenty-five years of the nineteenth century. Reparation for the Slave Trade became through his efforts, one of the dominant influences making for the support of Missions. Indeed, we may go further and claim that is was his insistence on this aspect which helped to swell the public support for the campaign for the ending of the Slave Trade and the abolition of slavery; created a public response later to the challenge of David Livingstone; and has ever since his time secured an alliance between specifically missionary organizations and those concerned with more limited humanitarian objectives—an alliance which has decisively shaped the whole missionary movement down until our own day.

Not unrelated to the previous motive, and possibly deriving from it, was the specifically religious co-efficient of that sense of political trusteeship which was noticed in the last chapter. We may note a missionary comment on the debate on

[16] Josiah Pratt quoted in *Proceedings of the Society for Missions to Africa and the East instituted by members of the Established Church* (London), vol. i (1801-1805), pp. 340-341.
[17] *Missionary Register*, 1813, p. 230.

the renewal of the East India Company's Charter in 1813, during which the issue of a Church Establishment in India was discussed and decided.

While the mercantile classes throughout the Empire are urging with earnestness, their claims to a share in the commerce of the East; every Briton, as a Christian, has a still higher object placed before him, and is now called to come forward, with all the influence he can exert to secure to sixty millions of British subjects in India, the means of hearing the Word of Life.[18]

There is a further interesting contemporary comment on that debate, a footnote so to speak, which records that 'Mr Wilberforce . . . declared, that in his opinion, independent of the cause of Christianity, the cause of humanity was more interested in this question than even in that of the Slave Trade.'[19]

Reparation for the past was yielding to trusteeship for the present and the future, a significant shift of emphasis which reflected itself increasingly in the public mind in this country in regard to Britain's overseas possessions. It is of some importance that the historian should keep in mind the fact that with the increasing sense of national pride which certainly burgeoned with Britain's victorious emergence from the Napoleonic wars, with her dominating commercial and industrial position, and with her acquisition of so many territories overseas, there was continually at work as a leaven in the nation a vocal minority which insisted that privilege meant stewardship. Self-interest was continually challenged by the demand for conduct worthy of a Christian nation. This can easily be

[18] *Missionary Register*, 1813, p. 114.
[19] *Missionary Register*, p. 236. The *Proceedings of the Church Missionary Society*, together with the *Missionary Register*, also published by the C.M.S., are primary sources of great importance for this period, for they were never limited to an exclusive concern for the activities of C.M.S., but contained much information from other sources, and commented freely on the activities of Parliament.

denounced as hypocrisy, and has been so denounced! Yet it remains that that is not the whole story. The integrity of countless administrators of the old colonial empire, and the high tradition of the Indian Civil Service, were not accidents. Nor can they be dismissed as a conventional veneer. They were deeply motivated by Christian convictions which first found overt expression in the campaign for the abolition of slavery and its parallel movement of missionary enthusiasm.

In the third place there was, as a missionary motive, a tremendous sense of gratitude for the Gospel. There is a continuous refrain in the sermons of the period, when concerned with the missionary enterprise, in the records of the proceedings of societies, and in private exhortations of friends, a refrain which runs 'Every blessing which you now enjoy whispers "Freely you have received freely give".' Sometimes the words run 'As you have received mercy, impart mercy'.

One typical illustration may suffice. In the *Evangelical Magazine* for 1794 there is an article with the curious title 'To the Evangelical Dissenters who practise Infant Baptism'. It is an outright appeal for support in the formation of a Missionary Society. Historically this article was one of the creative influences which went towards bringing into existence the London Missionary Society in 1795. The author, Dr David Bogue, began the article as follows:

> Christian Brethren,
> God has favoured us with the knowledge of the way of salvation through a crucified Redeemer. Our obligations to him on this account are inexpressible; and, I trust, we are often prompted from the fulness of our hearts to ask *what shall we render unto the Lord for all his benefits*.[20]

The article goes on to present the readers with a picture of the world in which half the human race are 'destitute of the

[20] Richard Lovett, *The History of the London Missionary Society* (Oxford University Press, 1899), p. 6.

knowledge of the Gospel'. It would not be unfair to say of all the missionary societies which in Britain were formed during this period that they were carried into existence on a tidal wave of gratitude to God for the Gospel, or as Van Den Berg puts it, as being 'constrained by Jesus' love'.

Coupled with this emphasis and perhaps as a *fourth* motive there was also a very profound theological sense of what was due to God's glory. In that same article Dr Bogue says

We all know that it is the supreme end of our existence to glorify God. But can we suppose that though we endeavour *personally* to live to His honour, our obligations are fulfilled, while we have employed no methods *as a Christian body* to lead our brethren in Pagan lands to glorify Him also, by making them acquainted with His nature, government, and grace?[21]

In the first issue of the *Missionary Register* in 1813 the Editor argues as the ground for the support of Missions that 'The honour of your Divine Master demands it at your hands'.[22]

As early as 1803, in one of the first annual sermons preached before the Church Missionary Society the Rev. Richard Cecil explicitly states as the primary ground for his appeal for support of the missionary cause 'The Glory of God.' And under this heading he began by saying:

On this ground let us join the universal Church in crying 'Thy Kingdom come'—in seeking to promote this Kingdom to the utmost of our power. . . .[23]

A final word as to motive must be said. Throughout the literature of our period, in so far as it touches on the genesis of the modern missionary movement, there is an overwhelming consensus about the obligation of Christians to obey the

[21] Richard Lovett, *op. cit.*, p. 7.   [22] *Missionary Register*, 1813, p. 5.
[23] Richard Cecil, *op. cit.*, p. 198.

divine commission. The main burden of William Carey's *Enquiry* is concerned with the relevance of St Matthew 28.19. That *Enquiry*, by the way, is a moving testimony to the total irrelevance of the theological debate as to whether those words represent the *ipsissima verba* of our Lord or are a later interpretation of his mind. Here, if ever, it is true—and our generation needs to remember, what our fathers never doubted—that all too easily:

> . . . the native hue of resolution
> Is sicklied o'er with the pale cast of thought,
> And enterprises of great pith and moment
> With this regard their currents turn awry,
> And lose the name of action.[24]

To which a preacher in the year 1805 can add this suitable aphorism: 'Success belongs to God—duty is our part'.[25]

A group of ministers in Warwickshire may speak for this whole generation when we overhear them debating on June 27, 1793 the question, 'What is the duty of Christians with respect of the spread of the Gospel?', and their resolving 'that it is the duty of all Christians to employ every means in their power to spread the knowledge of the Gospel both at home and abroad'.[26] That resolution led on directly to the foundation of the London Missionary Society.

In the material here presented I have tried to provide the basis upon which a fair assessment can be made of the motives which inspired the beginning of the modern missionary movement. I believe that I have accurately indicated the main stream of those convictions and insights which led these men, for the most part worthy but quite inconspicuous persons to

[24] William Shakespeare, *Hamlet* Act III Scene 1.
[25] John Venn preaching before the Church Missionary Society on June 4th, 1805.
[26] Richard Lovett, *op. cit.*, p. 12.

attempt such great designs at such an apparently unpropitious moment in history.

Arguing then from strength I will present the critic with another piece of evidence for his attack on missions. In the struggle to secure free entrance for missionaries into India, which as we have seen, was an issue intensely bound up with the renewal of the East India Company's Charter in 1813, one missionary leader could write:

Shall sixty million heathen subjects of the British crown . . . be abandoned to a cruel and debasing superstition, when prudent measures and holy men will, with the blessing of God, be the means of enlightening their minds, elevating their characters, attaching them to British interests, and everlastingly saving their souls?[27]

It is easy to make merry over those 'British interests'. Historical perspective, and a candid examination of all the evidence, will make clear that such expressions were designed primarily to turn the flank of commercial and political obstruction to any promotion of the missionary cause. The real motives of the missionary enterprise were such as have been indicated.

[27] *Missionary Register* 1813, pp. 115-116. It would be interesting to explore the relationship of the phrase 'attaching them to British interests' to much contemporary political thinking about the 'defence' of the Empire. See the chapter by David Fieldhouse in *Essays in Imperial Government*, edited by Kenneth Robinson and Frederick Madden (Oxford, Basil Blackwell, 1963), pp. 23-45.

3

CHRISTIANITY AND THE THIRD
BRITISH EMPIRE
1857-1947

A reasonable case can be made for saying that the *first* British Empire came to an end with the revolt of the American colonies. And the fact that the year 1776 also saw the publication of Adam Smith's *Inquiry into the Wealth of Nations*, a book which slowly worked a revolution in thinking about colonies, may serve to underline the nature of that first empire as being fundamentally commercial in character and inspiration.

That I should date the *third* British Empire from 1857 to 1947, the first date being that of the Indian Mutiny, might appear to suggest that I understand the period from 1776, or at least from the Treaty of Paris in 1781, until 1857 as being that of the *second* British Empire, itself brought to an end by a rebellion.

History is nothing like as tidy as that. What can best be described as the *second* British Empire was the development of a number of territories, settled by people of British stock, into a partnership between the United Kingdom and a number of self-governing dominions. This, by the way, was the only Empire that really engaged the devotion of Rudyard Kipling. His poem *The Young Queen*, written to celebrate the inauguration of the Commonwealth of Australia on New Year's Day, 1901, with its refrain of the 'Five free nations', or his poem *The Song of the Sons*, and those poignant verses about *The Native-Born*, express an emotion which was no mere sentiment, as was amply demonstrated on the battlefields of two World Wars.

The *third* British Empire, which is our present theme, refers to the dominion exercised by Britain over peoples of other racial stocks, of alien cultures, of different religious traditions. This Empire, too, has gone through many vicissitudes. But some claim can be made for the fact that its keynote has been a sense of trusteeship on the part of the ruling power. Substance can be given to that claim when it is remembered that since 1947 there have been thirteen meetings of Commonwealth Prime Ministers. In July, 1964 one such meeting was held at which, out of eighteen representatives of independent nations within the Commonwealth, only four were white. If British imperialism had really been as ghastly a tyranny as it is often represented as having been, it is very difficult to explain these meetings of Commonwealth Prime Ministers.

Only a brief word of explanation is needed of the dates chosen. 1857-1947. Once again they are not precise. If 1857 saw the winding up of the East India Company's rule, and the acceptance of full responsibility for India by the Government in London, the change was more significant from the point of view of London than of India. Arcot and Plassey had really decided who would rule India for the next two-hundred years. But the date, 1857, does mark an explicit acceptance of responsibility, the acceptance of a trust.

1947 saw the ending of that responsibility in the sub-continent. But this date is more in the nature of a symbol. It stands for the peaceful handing-over of the exercise of power, and in this respect was the pattern for all those other transfers of authority which have taken place since then.

Nineteenth Century Attitudes

Earlier I have indicated my conviction that there is no adequate understanding of the expansion of Christianity, no possibility of an intelligent appraisal of the missionary movement, which sees them out of relation to the currents of human thought and action in the political and economic fields. For our purpose it is very important to grasp what were the ideas about Empire which were effective in determining British policy in regard to the peoples of Asia and Africa who were under British rule.

In 1828 Huskisson addressed the House of Commons on civil government in Canada. What he said in regard to Canada, part of which has already been quoted is, however, of far wider reference:

We are not, Sir, at liberty to forego the high and important duties imposed upon us by our relative situation towards these colonies . . . We have everywhere displayed marks of paternal government, and planted improvement, not only on our colonies there, but wherever our Empire is acknowledged . . . Sir, England is the parent of many flourishing colonies . . . In every quarter of the globe we have planted the seeds of freedom, civilization and Christianity. To every corner of the globe we have carried the language, the free institutions, the system of laws, which prevail in this country . . . And if it be said by some selfish calculator that we have done all this at the expense of sacrifices, we are still the first and happiest people in the world.[1]

Professor Knorr, commenting on that speech, notes that it assumes three convictions. First, Great Britain has a duty to discharge towards her colonies. She must protect, supervise and assist them. Second, by virtue of her world-wide colonization, she is 'furthering the cause of freedom, peace, order and

---

[1] Robert Walsh, *op. cit.*, pp. 543 f.

Christian civilization'. Third, it is the privilege of Great Britain to accept tasks and duties even at the expense of sacrifices.[2]

We may, if we like, dismiss that speech as rhetoric, as playing to national prejudices, with an ear to the religious gallery. What is difficult is to fail to notice in his words echoes of sentiments which, in the last chapter, we saw were powerful incentives to missionary endeavour. We are coming to a period when the two streams, one of national expansion and the other of Christian outreach, were, at least in regard to the third British Empire, to flow side by side, and indeed frequently to coalesce. Which was to influence the other most it is impossible to say. If you stand at the confluence of the Blue and White Niles at Khartoum, you will see the remarkable sight of two rivers, differently coloured, meeting, running parallel to one another in the same river-bed, and finally coalescing. That is a very dangerous analogy, if pressed too far. In even making it I present a hostage to those who are only too eager to see Christian Missions as agents of imperialism. Yet I take the risk of being misunderstood and misrepresented. I do so because I am prepared to admit frankly the ambivalent nature of the Christian impact upon history.

It is impossible to read the records of the Evangelical Revival in England without being impressed by the deep seriousness which it engendered in many Englishmen, a seriousness which took the shape of a continual preoccupation with duty. From the second quarter of the nineteenth century this became a marked feature of leadership in every aspect of the national life. That duty and self-interest often coincided provided all that was necessary for the accusation of British hypocrisy. But duty no less often did, in fact, involve self-sacrifice. While admitting the one, we must admit both. Certain it is that in the speeches of Peel, Gladstone, Lord John

[2] Klaus Knorr, *op. cit.*, p. 366.

Russell and Earl Grey, and others like-minded, the accent is continually laid on duty, as though that could be assumed to clinch an argument. Before we dismiss the argument we must explain the assumption.

Earl Grey was Secretary of State for the Colonial Department in the Administration of Lord John Russell, 1846-1852. In his 'Preliminary Remarks', which introduce a volume of letters on Colonial policy, he says:

I conceive that, by acquisition of its Colonial dominions, the Nation has incurred a responsibility of the highest kind, which it is not at liberty to throw off. The authority of the British Crown is at this moment the most powerful instrument, under Providence, of maintaining peace and order in many extensive regions of the earth, and thereby assists in diffusing amongst millions of the human race, the blessings of Christianity and civilization. Supposing it was clear (which I am far from admitting) that a reduction of our national expenditure (otherwise impracticable), to the extent of a few hundred thousand a year, could be effected by withdrawing our authority and protection from our numerous Colonies, should we be satisfied, for the sake of such a saving, in taking this step, and thus abandoning this duty which seems to have been cast upon us?[3]

We will note there the confluence of the two streams, Empire and Christianity. We will also notice the close association of Christianity and Civilization, which had already appeared in Huskisson's speech in 1828. To the men of that generation, to the European man of the nineteenth century as a whole, the two were opposite sides of the same coin. It is very easy to dismiss this as cultural *hubris* and theological illiteracy. What we ought to recognize is that in this close association of ideas we are seeing the vestigial remains of Europe's mediaeval heritage of ideas, among them the idea of Christendom. The

[3] Earl Grey, *The Colonial Policy of Lord John Russell's Administration* (Richard Bentley, London, 1853), vol. i, pp. 13-14.

fact that today no one of us would make this equation, and that we are shocked that it was so continuously made in the nineteenth century, is some measure of how true it is that we live in a post-Christian era. It is no obvious mark of spiritual progress that, without any ignoring of other civilizations, few of us today would presume to talk about 'Christian Civilization' without being very nervous as to how soon the laughter would break out.

There was no such diffidence a century ago, as we have seen. This explains the unconscious arrogance, which would appear to be a national characteristic, perhaps hardly less evident in our contemporary mood of self-criticism than it was in the supremely un-self-critical mood aptly expressed in the following quotation from a speech of Gladstone's in 1855:

It is because we feel convinced that our Constitution is a blessing to us, and will be a blessing to our posterity . . . that we are desirous of extending its influence, and that it should not be confined within the borders of this little island; but that if it please Providence to create openings for us in the broad fields of distant continents, we shall avail ourselves in reason and moderation of those openings to reproduce the copy of those laws and institutions, those habits and national characteristics, which have made England so famous as she is![4]

A generation as suspicious as ours of all rhetoric, whether in the pulpit or the House of Commons, finds it easy to bandy about the word 'hypocritical' and to point to the manifold discrepancies between precept and practice. Yet there were men of action, the field-workers of empire who demonstrated in practice that duty was a word with a deep meaning, and one that could march with a great vision. Soon after the beginning of the nineteenth century we can see this combination at work in two of the East India Company's servants, men by no

[4] Paul Knaplund, *Gladstone and Britain's Imperial Policy* (Allen and Unwin, 1927), p. 203.

means exceptional either in their conception of duty or in their far-sightedness.

Thomas Munro, who worked successfully to establish a fair land settlement for the peasantry of the Madras area of the Company's responsibility, could see the goal of his work: 'Whenever we are obliged to resign our sovereignty we should leave the natives so far improved from their connection with us, as to be capable of maintaining a free, or at least a regular, government among themselves.' That day appeared to Munro to be a long way ahead. But he worked patiently towards it. Another servant of the Company, a generation younger than Munro, Elphinstone, whose service was in Western India, thought of British rule in India that 'the most desirable death for us to die should be the improvement of the nation reaching such a pitch as would render it impossible for a foreign nation to retain the Government'.[5]

Nor was that a view confined to the man who worked in India and loved his work and the people for whom he worked. Paternal his rule might be, and was, but running right through the pattern of nineteenth century empire, as far as Britain was concerned, was the thread, never broken, which betokened an inevitable end of imperial rule. On July 10th, 1833, Mr Charles Grant, President of the Board of Control of the East India Company, moved that the Bill for the better government of His Majesty's Indian territories should be read a second time. The motion was carried without a division but not without debate. In the course of this debate Macaulay made a speech in which the following passage occurs:

The destinies of our Indian empire are covered with thick darkness. It is difficult to form any conjecture as to the fate reserved for a State which resembles no other in history . . . The laws which regulate its growth and its decay are still unknown

[5] Philip Woodruff, *The Men Who Ruled India: The Founders* (Jonathan Cape, 1953), p. 14.

to us. It may be that the public mind of India may expand under our system till it has outgrown that system; that by good government we may educate our subjects into a capacity for better government; that, having become instructed in European knowledge, they may, in some future age, demand European institutions. Whether such a day will ever come I know not. But never will I attempt to avert or to retard it. Whenever it comes, it will be the proudest day in English history. . . .[6]

In his famous Minute on Indian Education, dated February 2nd, 1835, Macaulay sought to advance the date of that 'proudest day' by insisting on the need for English to be the medium of higher education in India. Not all his arguments would pass muster today. But there would seem to be no question that his influence to this end decisively shaped the future of India for India's good, and India's future independence.

Many factors were to operate to postpone the realization of the goal of independence until the patience of both the wards and the trustees was exhausted. Yet of India it can be fairly claimed that the dedication in Philip Woodruff's second volume of his study of the British rulers of India stands true. The dedication to that volume, entitled *The Founders*, reads:

> To the Peoples of India and Pakistan
> whose tranquillity was our care
> whose division is our failure
> and whose continuance
> in the family of nations to which we belong
> is our Memorial.

Words published in 1954 are still true in 1964, nearly twenty

[6] The full speech is published in *Speeches by Lord Macaulay with his Minute on Indian Education*, ed. G. M. Young, (Oxford University Press, 1935), p. 155. The link between Macaulay's Minute and the pioneer work of the Scots missionary Alexander Duff in regard to English as the medium of education, is well described in George Smith, *Alexander Duff* (Hodder and Stoughton, 1879), vol. i, pp. 104-205.

years after independence. Whatever the future holds, they bear witness to an achievement unique in the records of any empire of which we have knowledge.

Men Who Ruled Africa

What is very important for our understanding is that this tradition of a duty and a trust and a goal also inspired the best of those who, from the last twenty years of the nineteenth century, ruled for so short a time over vast areas of Africa. Once again historical perspective is called for. When the first Europeans penetrated beyond the coast-line of Africa they found people living in conditions about as remote from those in nineteenth-century Europe as could well be imagined. Large areas had been ravaged by the slave-trade. The peoples appeared to be primitive, their habits were savage, their language difficult to understand. There was no written literature, as none of the languages had been reduced to writing, and so there was no visible record of the past. Buildings were temporary; much of the country not ravaged by the slave-trade was ravaged by the tsetse fly and other insects. Life certainly seemed to be 'nasty, brutish and short'. Such was Africa as the white man first saw it. We know, today, that there was much more to Africa than the first adventurers understood, but those first explorers and administrators were not anthropologists, philologists or historians. What is so remarkable is that so many of them, in spite of what they thought they saw, had no doubts whatever of the infinite possibilities of the Africans. That this was the conviction of missionaries was natural, for otherwise they would never have gone to Africa. But it was also the conviction of empire-builders. As good an illustration of such men as any is Harry Johnston, born in London on June 12th, 1858. Johnston was to become with Cecil Rhodes and Frederick Lugard one of the three principal builders of Britain's African Empire. In passing it may be noted, as not wholly irrelevant, that in the case of Johnston and Lugard both came from devout Christian homes, Lugard's mother having herself been a missionary, his father an Army Chaplain in India.

1897, the year of the Jubilee of Queen Victoria, was perhaps the high peak of British Imperialism. It was, be it remembered also, the year which saw the publication of Kipling's *Recessional*, that solemn warning to all imperialists. In that year Johnston wrote from Nyasaland words which read curiously in this year 1964 which has seen Nyasaland become independent under the name of Malawi, words written just fifty years before 1947. 'Central Africa', he wrote, 'is probably as remote from self-government or representative institutions as is the case with India.' Then, after elaborating a favourite theme of his, that the Africans at that stage needed the help of the white man, he added:

Yet it must be borne in mind that the negro is a man with man's rights; above all that he was the owner of the country before we came; and deserves, nay, is entitled to, a share in the land commensurate with his needs and numbers; that in numbers he will always exceed the White man, while he may some day come to rival him in intelligence; and that finally, if we do not use our power to govern him with absolute justice the time will come sooner or later when he will rise against us and expel us as the Egyptian officials were expelled from the Sudan.[7]

In view of some quotations from Harry Johnston which will be given later, I have no doubt that, could he have foreseen the creation of Malawi under such far happier circumstances, he would have known how greatly this was due, not only to the justice of many administrators, but also to the missionary work of the Church of Scotland Mission and the Universities' Mission to Central Africa.

[7] Roland Oliver, *Sir Harry Johnston and the Scramble for Africa* (Chatto and Windus, 1957), pp. 258-259.

E

There is another pleasant glimpse of Johnston, this time in Uganda in 1900. He was visiting the Basoga people and to his missionary interpreter he said,

Tell them how interested the Queen is in their welfare, how she wants them to improve themselves and their country. We were like you long years ago, going about naked . . . with our war paint on, but when we learnt Christianity from the Romans we changed and became great. We want you to learn Christianity and follow our steps and you too will be great.[8]

We recognize there the authentic flavour of Victorian confidence, as yet untinged by the mood of Kipling's *Recessional*, but we should also note the sincerity of its recognition of the moral and religious basis of Empire. If I labour the point, it is because it is today so widely overlooked when not denied.

In 1920, towards the end of his life, with his great career behind him, Johnston ends one of his books with some words we can appreciate in their full painfulness as a prophecy, all too likely to be fulfilled.

White people must try to realize that the still Backward races, the once decrepit nations, have travelled far in intellectuality since the middle of the nineteenth century, and that the continuance of an insulting policy towards them will join them some day in a vast league against Europe and America, which will set back the millennium and perhaps even ruin humanity in general. Nature will have conquered by setting one half of mankind against the other.[9]

Some of the greatest empire-builders were men most deeply aware of the perils of *hubris*.

Meanwhile, less prophetic minds, though not less conscientious, were concerned to temper the wind of change to the imperfectly prepared peoples of Africa. This was at least part,

[8] Roland Oliver, *op. cit.*, p. 297.
[9] H. H. Johnston, *The Backward People and our Relations with Them* (Oxford University Press, 1920), p. 61.

a genuine part, of the policy of Indirect Rule, associated with the name of Lugard. The policy can perhaps be summarized in a sentence which does not wholly fail to do justice to a deep sense of responsibility. The goal was this: 'An ordered society of status rather than contract was to be preserved, in which a paternalistic British Government should provide the superior level, regulating the pace and nature of change, economic, social and political.[10] When in Kenya in 1907 a suggestion was made that unofficial trustees might be appointed to advise on African interests, Winston Churchill, then Under-Secretary of State for the Colonies, not uncharacteristically remarked that 'the government . . . in this matter, as in all others affecting the welfare of the natives, would act as their trustees'.[11]

Three years later, in less pontifical mood, the Governor of Kenya, Sir Percy Girouard, suggested that in connection with the controversial moving of the Masai tribe to new lands, unofficial trustees should be appointed 'say two bishops and the Secretary of native affairs'. He was overruled by the Secretary of State, Lord Crewe, who referred back to Mr Churchill's pronouncement. In 1923, however, these pronouncements, while not forgotten, were in practice set aside when a missionary was appointed to the Legislative Council 'to represent native interests', though the Government safeguarded its position by distinguishing between 'native interests' and the natives themselves. Paternalism was still the rule. The fact that a missionary could be so appointed, soon to be joined by others, is an interesting illustration of our analogy of the White and the Blue Nile.[12]

'Lay' Christianity in the Empire

Before we turn to the more explicit influence of the mis-

[10] Kenneth Robinson and Frederick Madden, *Essays in Imperial Government*, (Basil Blackwell, Oxford, 1963), p. 63.
[11] *Ibid.*, p. 142.　　[12] *Ibid.*, p. 144.

sionary movement in British territories[13] during this period, some further evidence must be drawn upon to show how there was within the imperial development during these years a widely diffused Christian influence, none the less influential, for being 'lay' in character and rarely dogmatic in expression. It was the lay counterpart of the more specifically denominational approach of the Missions.

Already as far back as 1769 in Bengal John Shore, later to become Lord Teignmouth, was marked as a 'serious man' in the Evangelical tradition. Less articulate, yet profoundly religious, were those servants of the East India Company such as we have already noticed, Munro and Elphinstone. These were followed by men of a fiercer breed, to match perhaps a fiercer situation. The Lawrences, Montgomery, Sir Herbert Edwardes, men of an uncompromisingly Evangelical turn of speech and behaviour, gave themselves unsparingly and conscientiously to the service and salvation of India. And by salvation they meant religious salvation as they understood it. Harsh their creed may seem to us, but fundamentally they were harsh with themselves first of all. Perhaps the best tribute to the inner quality of these men comes in Philip Woodruff's chapter on 'The Titans of the Punjab' in his book *The Founders*.

Few of these men were married; they speak constantly of their mothers in terms as emotional as they use of their religion. Passion belonged in them and was harnessed to work and to bodily rigour. A man who wished for marriage before middle-age was frowned on: it was an infidelity to the ideal of work. Still there were marriages; there were deaths too among the wives and many among the children. Even those who lived paid a price. A woman who married into the Punjab Commission had taken a step as decisive as entering a convent. She and her children

[13] Some intriguing parallels can be discovered in *Missionaries, Chinese and Diplomats: The American Protestant Missionary Movement in China, 1890-1952* by Paul A. Varg (Princeton University Press, 1958).

became camp equipment, jolted in bullock-carts and on the backs
of camels, exposed to dust, sun, heat, cholera, malaria, moving
always from tent to bungalow and back again, gypsies without
a home beneath the stars. They must expect hard wear and a
short life and in the end, if they survived, years of deadening
separation. To accept such a life without some sense of spiritual
dedication would almost inevitably mean a coarsening of the
fibres, but the wives of the Lawrences and their followers were
vowed to God just as definitely as their husbands, were as far from
humanity, as closely knit in a community of work and religion.[14]

The relentless self-denial of the anchorites of the desert, the
first Benedictines, the early friars, the Jesuits of Upper Canada,
the Moravians, and an inner flame of devotion common to
them all, found its nineteenth century parallel not only among
missionaries but also in this giant breed who, in India, presi-
ded over the transfer of power from the East India Company
to the Imperial Government. Nor did this tradition ever
wholly die out. In 1902, writing to her friend Moberley Bell,
Lady Lugard could say of her husband, whose life she wholly
shared:

Sir Frederick has nearly killed himself—and I think a fair
proportion of his staff too—with overwork. Yet they like it. After
all they are working for an idea, and that is more than all men
can say.[15]

No one who knew Lord Lugard would doubt the religious
content of his devotion to hard work. He might express himself with more restraint than an Edwardes or a Lawrence, but
the inheritance is unmistakable.

Meanwhile, another stream of 'lay' Christianity began to
flow out into the work of administering the Empire. The
source of this stream was the direct influence of Dr Arnold

[14] Philip Woodruff, *op. cit.*, p. 325.
[15] Margery Perham, *Lugard: The Years of Authority, 1898-1945* (Collins,
1960), p. 81.

of Rugby upon the English public school system. That system is under attack today, but I am here concerned solely with Dr Arnold's influence on the men who ruled the 'Third British Empire', and the extent of that influence cannot be exaggerated. Indeed, most historians readily acknowledge that Dr Arnold's development of the prefectorial system was singularly well adapted to train the men who were to be the future rulers of primitive peoples. Certain it is that for the best part of one hundred years the great majority of the administrators and educationists of the Colonial Empire came from schools where curriculum and ethics had been profoundly affected by Dr Arnold. The fact that the Sudan, during the Condominium, was 'a land of the "blacks" ruled by "blues"' was near enough to the truth. Nearer still would it be true of the Sudan, and of all former British Tropical Africa, that they were ruled by the 'old school-tie'.

There is an interesting description of such men in a recent essay on 'Indirect Rule in Northern Nigeria, 1906-11'.

Once the South African war ended Northern Nigeria provided one of the more attractive fields for the adventurous spirits amongst the products of the public schools and Universities. These men were prepared to devote themselves to their careers, endure discomforts and disease, learn African languages, tour remote and dangerous districts, and aim at understanding the African way of life. They felt themselves capable of deciding how far that way of life should be preserved, and how far altered in the interests of justice and civilization. If they accepted the principle of ruling indirectly, it was certainly in no spirit of *laissez-faire*.[16]

Dr Arnold's explicit objective, pursued with unflagging zeal, was an education which would produce what he called 'Christian gentlemen'. This is no place to argue the adequacy of that

[16] Mary Bull in *Essays in Imperial Government*, p. 49.

definition as a goal of education. Of it two things may be said, and they are very important for our subject. In the first place the goal was surprisingly often realized. Many of the rulers of this Third Empire were quite explicitly and unashamedly Christians and their regular attendance at worship, where it was possible, was no conventional conformity. It was no idiosyncrasy which led a young political officer in the Sudan to produce his own collection of prayers, some in my present possession, for use by little groups of Christians in the political service who might be far from any of the regular ministrations of their Church. I remember well as a young missionary myself, in Northern Nigeria, being challenged one day by a senior British official as to how I had spent the time before breakfast, and feeling both rebuked and impressed when told that he regularly spent that time reading his New Testament in the Hausa vernacular. These men were not exceptions. They were far more typical than many people realize. Had they not been so, the end of the third British Empire would have followed a very different course from that which we have seen.

In 1839 occurred the first Afghan war which Philip Woodruff describes as 'less defensible on moral grounds than any in our history in India—and not only that but less successful'. He goes on to record that

even at such a time, the signature of an Englishman promising to pay the bearer in India would pass as currency in an Afghan bazaar, though the writer might be shut up in a dungeon, his one shirt soaked in dried blood and lousy with vermin.[17]

When Edwardes was enforcing British ideas of order among the Pathans of the Northwest frontier, the question could seriously be asked by Waziri tribesmen, 'Was it true, as they had heard, that the English suffered from a strange affliction which made them unable to lie?'[18] If for a long time that

[17] Philip Woodruff, *op. cit.*, p. 326.   [18] Philip Woodruff, *op. cit.*, p. 332.

tradition held, it was due to Dr Arnold more than to any other single man.

One by-product of this influence must be noted. During the period we are considering, a great many of those missionaries who were raised to the Anglican episcopate in dioceses in Asia and Africa, as well as those thus appointed direct from England, had themselves been educated at those same public schools. The interplay of influence between missionary leaders and government officials offers a fascinating subject for research. The influence of this informal and strictly unofficial relationship, born of a common educational background, has still to be assessed. It was certainly considerable in both directions.

Missionaries and Governments

Against the background which I have described, the background of certain ideas of Empire, and the background of this diffused, but not the less real influence of Christian thinking and Christian action, we can the better get in perspective the explicit missionary activity of the Christian Church.

Important as it is to see the missionary movement in a real relationship with other contemporary activities, we shall note the unequivocal testimony of Professor Knorr when he says:

Although the missionary movement was loosely connected with the European penetration of non-European continents, in England it was totally dissociated from the Government. Unwittingly it may have assisted British colonial expansion, but it never intended to do so during the period under consideration. Former systems of government-assisted and directed missionary enterprises were sharply rejected.[19]

That judgment can, perhaps, stand, though a qualification will be indicated later. Essentially the missionary movement was concerned to proclaim the Christian Gospel, invite men

[19] Klaus Knorr, *op. cit.*, p. 381.

and women to accept Jesus Christ as Saviour and Lord, and enter into discipleship. The 'how' of the proclamation, the form of the 'invitation', the 'way' of discipleship might be presented in differing fashions. On the subject of the main intention there was no divergence. It was this which gave the missionary movement its penetrating power, made it, at the best of times, an uneasy partner even with sympathetic governments and, as we shall see in a subsequent chapter, stimulated resistance. The last century and a half has seen considerable changes of vocabulary. There is today a more respectful attitude towards the ancient religious cultures of the East and of Africa than obtained at the beginning of our period. There is again a greater humility on the part of Western missionaries due to a franker acknowledgment of the corruptions of Western civilization. Yet whatever changes all this may involve in missionary method, the direction and purpose of the missionary movement remains anchored to the New Testament commission and the Biblical understanding of the nature and purpose of God for all mankind.

A subordinate feature of this primary intention was the setting up of Church structures wherever the proclamation of the Gospel evoked response. Suffice it now to note that, whatever the expression given to it, there was always present a belief that the form of the Church was part of the Church's Gospel. Most often this took the form of extending to Asia and Africa the denominational patterns with which the missionaries were familiar. And here must be included the one qualification I would wish to make to Professor Knorr's testimony. As regards India it was clearly seen by those who wished to open up that country to Christian missionary effort, that the only way to do so was by attempting an ecclesiastical establishment. This explains why, in 1813, the renewal of the Charter of the East India Company included provision for an establishment consisting of a bishop and three archdeacons to be paid for out of the Indian revenues of the Company. This 'Establishment' came to include as well provision for some ministers of the Church of Scotland. Primarily the purpose of the Establishment in India, as far as the intentions of the British Parliament were concerned, was to provide for the spiritual needs of the European population. Nevertheless it must be recognized that missionaries, aiming at the conversion of Hindus and Muslims, gained entry under this constitutional enactment although, and it is an important distinction, they were not covered by the financial arrangements. This 'Establishment' was to remain substantially financed out of the revenues of the Government of India down to 1947. The missionaries on the other hand were wholly financed by the voluntary contributions of the supporters of the Missionary Societies. Inherent in this arrangement was a dichotomy which was to have serious spiritual consequences. But that is another story. Candour, however, demands that this qualification to Professor Knorr's statement be registered.

Meanwhile it is probably true to say that the ordinary working missionary took his particular Church traditions very largely for granted. It was the only Church Order he knew and he brought it with him. His main concern was to communicate the Gospel with which he believed himself to be in trust.

The records make it clear that there were two main means of communication. The first of them was education. In almost every place illiteracy was the first problem to be tackled. Elementary education was, in practice, the foundation upon which the whole expansion of Christianity was built up. With this would often go technical education of a simple kind designed to raise the economic level of the people. Gradually higher education was attempted. West Africa, through Fourah Bay College, Sierra Leone, founded in 1827, slightly ante-dated those developments in India which are associated with Macaulay's Minute, and the pioneer work of Alexander Duff.

Of the significance of this aspect of missionary work, two appraisals of an objective kind may be quoted. The first comes from the report of the Commission on Higher Education in West Africa, a commission whose Chairman was the Right Hon. Walter Elliott. The report was published in 1945. It said:

> When one looks for the root from which West African education sprang one comes back, everywhere and always, to the missionaries. It was the Christian missions who first came out to the Coast without desire for fee or reward. It was the congregations in Britain and America who provided the first development funds, the pennies of poor people, expended without reckoning of capital or interest . . . It was, and still is, the Churches, who have made it possible to talk of West African education, higher, middle or lower, as a fact and not merely as an ideal.[20]

The same claims could be made for the rest of the Colonial Empire in Africa, and even to a very significant degree in the sub-continent of India during a large part of our period.[21]

A much more intriguing comment, one showing a more penetrating awareness of the real significance of the missionary movement, came from the pen of Sir Harry Johnston. Writing in *Views and Reviews*, in 1912, he says:

> The idea that there would ever be any serious demand on the part of the colonial peoples for a voice in their own taxation and government scarcely disturbed the forecast of any average imperialist . . . But unfortunately for the ideals of the imperialist Britain of twenty years ago, education was permeating the British Empire in all directions . . . Missionary Societies were everywhere founding schools, colleges and universities, attempt-

---

[20] *Report* Cmd. 6655 (H.M. Stationery Office, London, 1945), p. 16.
[21] The encouragement by the Government of India of higher education in English was welcomed immediately by the Missionary Societies which, to a large extent, were its pioneers.

ing to make black, brown and yellow peoples think and act like white Christians . . . impressing on them over and over again that once they were Christians and civilized, or even civilized without being Christian, they were the equal of any man, no matter of what colour or race.[22]

The date of that observation is interesting, as is his reference to the imperialism of the Jubilee generation. What is important is his recognition of the major part played by the missionary movement in putting ideas into peoples' heads. It was those who were singing the *Magnificat* in their hearts, and not the chanters of the *Internationale*, who were the real generators of that creative upsurge of the peoples of Asia and Africa which is the predominant political fact of our time. That is a thought to give us pause—and hope.

The *second* main instrument of communication, revolutionary in its insistence on the value of the individual person, was the mission hospital. Over a very large part of Asia and Africa during our period, Western scientific medicine, and the first attack on the sources of disease, were introduced by doctors and nurses in the service of the missionary societies.

In addition, and by no means to be underestimated, there have been the responsibilities accepted by many missionaries abroad, and by the committees of missionary societies at home, to be continually alert to the need to challenge governments to take the role of trusteeship seriously. During the greater part of the period from 1857-1947, at least in the British Colonial Empire of Africa, the essential and primary role of the Government was to establish peace and preserve order. The amelioration of life was, until after the first World War, left largely to the missionary societies, with some rare and distinguished exceptions, such as the Gordon College at Khartoum. The record of what missionaries, and missionary

[22] H. H. Johnston, *op. cit.*, pp. 232-234, quoted by Roland Oliver, *Sir Harry Johnston and the Scramble for Africa*, p. 352.

committees, did in this regard is a by no means undistinguished one, the story of which is still to be told.

I end this chapter, however, on a sober note and quote from Bishop Stephen Neill's *A History of Christian Missions*. At the end of a very searching summing-up on the subject of colonialism, he writes:

And finally comes religious aggression. For, say what we will, Christian missionary work is frequently understood by the peoples of Africa and the East not as the sharing of an inestimable treasure, but as an unwanted imposition from without, irreparably associated with the progress of the colonial powers.

He adds, and I would echo him:

How far this unfavourable judgment is justified we shall have later to consider; it needs to be stated . . . as part of the history, and part of the tragedy, of Christian Missions in the great century of Europe.[23]

---

[23] S. C. Neill, *op. cit.* (Penguin Books, 1964), p. 250.

4

THE DISINTEGRATING IMPACT
OF WESTERNIZATION

In the first three chapters I have tried to approach my subject historically, and I list in the bibliography sources from which my own judgments can be very easily checked, supplemented or corrected. My interpretation of the evidence may have gone wrong, but at least the evidence is available in very great volume. In this and in the subsequent chapters we move into a realm in which, inevitably, we find that we are more immediately involved ourselves and more likely to be influenced by subjective judgments. Ideas about imperialism may have been rightly or wrongly presented but, at least as far as Britain and France, Holland and Belgium are concerned, their imperialisms belong to history. They have been amply documented and can be analysed. A measure of perspective about them is possible.

> Lo, all our pomp of yesterday
> Is one with Nineveh and Tyre.

Far otherwise is the subject of this chapter. While we must look back and see how the disintegration of ancient cultures began, and what was the nature of the West's impact, yet this can be no mere historical study. For every day of the week our newspapers carry evidence of it from Asia and Africa. Without some understanding of what the impact of westernization has been and is, and indeed may be expected to continue to be, we cannot begin to understand what is happening in the world of our time.

Definition of Terms

By 'disintegration' I mean the break-up of those custom-dominated cultures in which the pace of change was so slow that it is reasonable to speak of their orders of society as static. Such were, in large measure, the custom-dominated cultures of Asia and Africa before the impact of westernization. Change, of course, there was. Africa, for instance, has from time immemorial seen countless migrations. Communities dissolved and crystallized again in new patterns. Yet, for all the movement of life, the overall picture is of an unchanging subsistence economy and a social structure everywhere dominated by kinship. It was a society in which a man's status was determined at birth. In India, even when every allowance has been made for successive invasions from Central Asia, each bringing in new influences, we find that society was rigidly controlled by caste. And caste was expressly designed to make social change extremely difficult. If in China society was differently organized from that of India, yet its own social organization was essentially conservative.

If we dwell on this fact of the slow tempo of change in Asia and Africa prior to the impact of the West, it is only by way of contrasting the pace of events before and after that impact. However strong may be the conservative forces in any given society today—and caste is still tenacious in its hold on Indian society, while kinship remains a living force in Africa, even in many of its towns and cities—yet no one can doubt the force of the impact made by the West, or fail to recognize the new tempo of change. And the effect of the new tempo of change is to disintegrate the old patterns of society, political, economic, social and religious. China and Japan are the two most dramatic illustrations of such a disintegration of the old ways of life in Asia. Lagos, Leopoldville, Lusaka and Johannesburg are a few instances of what is happening in Africa. Most vivid, because more instantaneous, for the tens of thousands of people dispossessed of their land, are such enterprises as the Kariba, Volta and High Assuan dams.

The point does not need arguing. But if the word 'disintegration' can be accepted, what is meant by 'westernization'? Here we need to be cautious. In many respects the peoples of Asia and Africa are as critical of the West as they are resentful of it, even when they want the benefits of its technology. In particular they resent the arrogant way in which we assume that democracy, for instance, is only democracy if it is *our* form of democracy. The African is fully entitled to insist that his method of 'palaver', by which a unanimous opinion is arrived at after long and patient discussion, is just as democratic as, if not more democratic than, the counting of heads and making the decision depend on a majority opinion. Parliamentary democracy, using the device of Her Majesty's loyal Opposition has been evolved in the West, but that is not the only form of democracy. It may even be doubted whether our English model can successfully be exported. As a word 'westernization' then must be used without the least hint that, in the realm of moral and spiritual values, there is something inherently superior about the Western way of life. To think so is to be guilty of a vulgar parochialism.

Yet the term 'westernization' is convenient if we use it primarily to cover that process of change which deals with every kind of human poverty—material poverty, poverty of skills, poverty of health, poverty of understanding. These are poverties with which Asia and Africa have been long acquainted, and from which they are seeking deliverance. It is in its capacity to help achieve this deliverance that 'westernization' is welcomed, and the word can thus be used without any reflection on the peoples of Asia and Africa.

If that be allowed, then we can accept the interpretation of 'westernization' given by Maurice Zinkin:

> The steady reduction of poverty which has characterized the West in the last century and a quarter is . . . unique in history. Its uniqueness is not, however, in all probability, the result of accident. Rather is it a result of the coming together in Western society of a whole series of institutions and attitudes, all of which were necessary to the nineteenth century's outburst of economic activity.
>
> It is, therefore, *a priori* likely that any underdeveloped society which wishes to develop will have to transform itself to be as like as possible in attitudes and institutions to Western Europe and its offshoots.[1]

That remains a very formidable statement to make. If it is true then the attack on poverty, poverty in its many-sidedness, must be a disintegrating process for those institutions and attitudes which have for so long prevented Asia and Africa from grappling with their poverty. It must likewise have its own direct bearing on our appraisal of the Christian missionary enterprise. Sociologically speaking, Christian Missions have been a disintegrating influence in Asia and Africa in proportion as they have successfully played their part in this attack on poverty. Whether it was ever possible for them to avoid being a disintegrating influence in other respects, is a wide question which must engage our attention in due course. For the present it is sufficient to note that already we have arrived at the point when we can see that 'disintegration' is not a negative term but may be an indispensable contribution towards a positive result.

There are four convenient aspects under which our subject can be studied—the political, the economic, the social, and the religious. These can be distinguished in some measure for

---

[1] Maurice Zinkin, *Development for Free Asia* (Chatto and Windus, 1956), p. 99.

F

purposes of analysis. But all the while we must bear in mind that in custom-controlled religious cultures of the types prevalent in Asia and Africa, it is, strictly speaking, impossible to distinguish between them. But that is only the obverse side of the underlying argument of these lectures, that the expansion of Christianity has never been a movement of pure spirit. Always and everywhere it has been inextricably bound up with the political, economic and social thinking which was its historical context at any one moment. This in no way invalidates our claim for the authentic truth of the Christian Faith. But it does demand that we examine the words 'Church History' as designating a proper subject of study, and discard them in favour of the more accurate term 'the Church in history'. If the doctrine of the Incarnation has to be safeguarded from our ever-present tendency towards docetism, so must the doctrine of the Church be protected from the same tendency. The study of the missionary movement in modern history is a sure prophylactic for this purpose. In this, as in all respects, what St Paul said of the Gospel is true for us, as it was for our fathers, that 'we have this treasure in earthen vessels, that the exceeding greatness of the power may be of God, and not from ourselves'.[2]

Another sobering consideration is provided by a modern historian, I. R. Sinai:

A new civilization can never arise without the disintegration of the old one. And this process of rebirth, this intervening period of deep crisis, the precondition for the creation of a new society capable of coping with the immense problems of the twentieth century, is a prolonged and stormy process which by its very nature will have to stretch over many generations, and even then suffer all the distortions and corruptions to which every human effort is heir.[3]

[2] II Cor. 4.7. RV.
[3] I. R. Sinai, *The Challenge of Modernization: The West's Impact on the Non-Western World* (Chatto and Windus, 1964), p. 58.

Political Change

A consideration of the *political* impact of the West on Asia and Africa may well start with the frank acknowledgment that, viewed politically, the impact was in no way concerned to relieve Asia and Africa of their poverty. It was mainly concerned with increasing the wealth of the West. Japan was opened at gun point by the Americans because they wanted to trade with Japan. China was forced by the nefarious opium war to open the treaty ports to Western occupation and to allow the principle of extra-territoriality to restrict her sovereignty. India was progressively overrun by British armies in order to protect areas already under British control. Britain took control of Uganda, Nigeria and Kenya primarily to anticipate the intrusion of other European powers. The part played by Christian opinion in England may have been decisive in encouraging Lugard to work for a British Protectorate over Uganda[4], just as Christian influences were active in securing the maintenance of a naval squadron on the West African coast to prevent the slave traffic, and so indirectly led to the establishment of British spheres of influence in West Africa. But, by and large, the political impact of the West was the impact of naked force seeking economic advantage for the particular nation in the West which had the most power available where it was needed.

And this exercise of political power disintegrated the old political traditions. In Japan the Shogunate gave way successively to an experiment in liberal democracy, then to an effective military dictatorship, and then, in 1945, to the virtual abdication by the Emperor of his primary role as the divine source of all social order in the nation, with the consequent establishment of the whole apparatus of a western state. In

[4] Margery Perham, *Lugard*, vol. i: *The Years of Adventure 1858-1898* (Collins, 1956), pp. 387-431.

China the reaction of a proud people was to overthrow its own ruling dynasty, to repudiate the age-long tradition of administration by an intellectual elite, and, after an attempt at western democracy, to accept, in its most rigid form, western-style Communism.

In India virtual anarchy was replaced after the Mutiny by British rule. The successor states of India and Pakistan are both modern states, quite unlike any previous form of rule known in the sub-continent.

In Africa tribal organization, whether it was expressed in the rule of a paramount chief, or of tribal elders, has everywhere given way to a new pattern of political control which is fundamentally different from anything known in the old Africa.

None of these illustrations is meant to imply that the future may not see even more dramatic changes. All that they illustrate is the disintegrating impact of the West on the old political order. But when it is remembered that the old political order was always assumed to be in some real sense religious, the overthrow of that old order was bound to have far-reaching effects on the peoples of the countries concerned. The psychic security of the people was undermined. This has proved to be a far more significant fact in the history of the past fifty years than is commonly recognized. One of the basic problems confronting all the independent nations of Asia and Africa is that of finding an adequate substitute for the sanction of religion as the ultimate ground of governmental authority. That may seem a strange statement to make in the second half of the twentieth century. But it is not so strange when we reflect on the time of troubles which ensued when in Europe the 'Divine Right of Kings' was called in question. Certainly in Asia and Africa some sense of divinity 'hedged' the ruler until the arrival of the western powers. With their departure an alternative has to be found. The ability to conquer poverty will *de facto* be accepted as warrant that the 'Mandate of Heaven' has been conferred. It remains to be seen if that 'Mandate' can be seen to be conferred otherwise than through Communism. And Communism, be it remembered, has considerable claims to be considered as a religion! That is just one insight into the political context of modern missions.

Economic Change

Psychic insecurity follows for any community when an age-old religion-based source of authority is suddenly replaced by a new centre of power. This is certainly a factor for which allowance must be made when studying the inner meaning of those influences which shape the corporate thinking of large masses of people. But the individual will often not be immediately conscious of the change. And he may, indeed, as far as his material comfort is concerned, appreciate the benefits conferred by the new ruler. An alien rule, if it can ensure order in place of anarchy, is often welcome for the time-being.

But if political change may be slight in its immediate impact on the individual, it is far otherwise with *economic* change. The disintegrating effect of economic change is often immediate and may be catastrophic in its impact on the individual.

This can be seen perhaps most clearly if we consider the imposition of taxation by the new ruler. Taxation, of course, was not a novelty in Asia. The novelty lay in its efficient application.

One illustration of the far-reaching changes imposed by Western ideas of efficiency can be seen in the land settlement of Bengal which influenced British practice all over India. The East India Company early took over from the effete Mogul power the task of raising taxes in Bengal. It found in operation a system which was chaotic and open to almost infinite abuse, being based on the age-old custom of farming out the responsibility for the collection of tax. Over the generations the tax-farmers had established themselves as large land-owners, though without any title. The peasants were still free peasants, although hopelessly indebted in many cases to the tax-farmers. The East India Company swept this system away, recognized the tax-farmers' legal right to the land, and almost with the stroke of a pen, reduced multitudes of peasants to the condition of landless serfs, tenants-at-will, of the large land-owners.[5]

This was a drastic change and helped to fasten even more firmly in the Indian villager that sense of apathy and hopelessness which has to this day proved so resistant to any new ideas.

Far more drastic was the incidence of taxation in Africa. In tribal Africa, where land was for the most part communally owned by the tribe, and where there was, except in a few areas, no money economy at all, taxation made drastic inroads on the old economy. Taxation was imposed by the foreign ruler to help pay for the administration of the area. But the African had no money. So he was compelled, in practice, to go and work in the mines or on the plantations which foreign entrepreneurs had created. This in turn meant absence from the tribal land for long periods at a time. Mines and plantations might be great distances from the individual labourer's home. A whole chain reaction of results followed. Many of them were social, as we shall see, but the main fact was the gradual separation of the man from his land, and that meant separation from the tribal economy. From being a man whose status was given him by virtue of his place in the councils of the tribe, he became a contract labourer.[6]

[5] S. Gopal, *The Permanent Settlement in Bengal and its Results* (Allen and Unwin, 1949).

[6] One vivid illustration of what this means by way of disintegrating the old political pattern of tribal life can be found in *Social Change in Modern Africa*, ed. Aidan Southall (Oxford University Press, 1961), p. 72, where the organization of the workers in the mines is shown to be quite unrelated to tribal patterns of authority.

All over Africa the organization of society slowly but surely moved from that of a society built on status, to a society built on contract. The African was, and often is still, very unwilling to abandon the old way for the new, but he was in this respect compelled to join the western economic order. This meant, among other things, that in ever-increasing numbers he became a city-dweller. That the African villager still represents the vast majority of the African population is true. That directly you go half-a-mile off any main road in Africa you find yourself in what is apparently still the old Africa is also true. But it is true only in its 'seeming'. That village which looks so traditional is geared in its life to the nearest town or city. Its young men and women, if they have not already gone to the town, want to go. And the goods available in the town are increasingly finding their way into the villages, and with the goods come new ways of thinking. An agricultural revolution is already in progress which, if it is less striking than the industrial revolution as seen in the mine-townships, is fully as significant. Indeed, its tempo may be expected to increase, for the population explosion is a fact in Africa, as elsewhere, and not only has the country population to be fed but so has the ever-growing population of the towns.

This is bound to mean a radical change in the whole economic ordering of society. It will become, and is already becoming increasingly impossible for the individual and his family to live off their own small share of the common land. A planned economy for a whole area will be essential if famine is to be avoided. And a planned economy calls for western institutions and attitudes wholly alien to the traditional society of Africa.

In passing, it may be noted as bearing on our general subject that the Church came into being in most of Africa while its ancient tribal and rural culture was at yet undisturbed. The Church in Africa is still overwhelmingly rural in its thinking and outlook; its clergy are, for the most part, peasants who have no understanding whatever of the problems of urban society. Time will remedy this; but the present moment is a moment of crisis for the Church in Africa, because the centre of power in the newly independent nations of Africa rests with those who live in, and control, the life of its cities. At few points is the contrast between the spread of Christianity in the first century and its spread in the nineteenth and early twentieth centuries as dramatic as in this distinction between a movement which concentrated on the cities, as did St Paul and others, and a movement which necessarily concentrated on the villages. This should warn us against giving much value to criticisms of the modern missionary movement in the light of St Paul's supposed missionary methods. As criticisms of the past they are almost wholly irrelevant. What is possible is that the new Africa and Asia, with their great development of cities, and the widespread influence of ideas current in cities, may provide circumstances in which some of St Paul's practice may achieve a new relevance. What is quite certain is that St Paul is no more to be conceived of as a missionary theoretician than he is to be interpreted as a systematic theologian. He was an opportunist for the Gospel. We need to be like him in that respect.

Meanwhile, this economic revolution, while undoubtedly disintegrating old ways of organizing the economy of society, should be seen as holding within it the prospects of a new integration of human life. It is to be viewed as a great constructive revolution.[7] Some words of I. R. Sinai's are relevant

[7] An admirable illustration of this will be found in 'Livingstonia as an Industrial Mission, 1875-1900: A Study of Commerce and Christianity in Nyasaland', by Kenneth J. McCracken; and in 'The Foundation of the Blantyre Mission, Nyasaland', by Andrew C. Ross. These two papers were published in *Religion in Africa*, Proceedings of a Seminar held in the Centre of African Studies, University of Edinburgh, April 10-12, 1964.

here. Referring immediately to Asia, what he says is as true of Africa, that

In these parts of the world, nature was more than man could cope with . . . Against the overwhelming hostility of physical environment, man was overshadowed and frustrated in all his efforts. In these extreme zones, man did not come to free movement. He could not find or gain freedom within himself, against the majestic and malignant pressure of his natural environment.[8]

Sinai there exposes the inner secret of why change in Asia and Africa has been so slow. He also explains why 'westernization', bringing with it the vast scope of its technology, makes possible rapid change. And herein lies the source of that dramatic alteration in the view point of multitudes in Asia and Africa, from hopelessness and apathy to a fierce hope. What we are seeing before our eyes is a revolution of expectancy. And that expectancy is full of a vast impatience. If we underrate that impatience, and that expectancy we shall find that our newspapers, for as far ahead as we can see, will yield nothing but one unpleasant surprise after another. 'Humanity', as General Smuts said prophetically fifty years ago, 'has struck its tents and is on the march'.

There is no putting-back of the clock. But, as Christians seeking to understand the missionary movement not only of the past but of the present and the future, we need to view soberly what all this means for the spirit of man. Only so will we correctly appraise the dimensions of our missionary duty.

Social Change

It must be obvious that political and economic changes, as outlined here, must have involved far-reaching changes in the whole fabric of society. Exhaustive work has been done on this subject by many distinguished social-anthropologists, and re-

[8] I. R. Sinai, *op. cit.*, p. 29.

ference to some of these studies will be found in the bibliography. Here we must consider three aspects of *social* change which are the necessary sequel to what we have already considered under the heads of political and economic change. There are many others which any student of sociology will recognize. To these three I will add a subject not yet considered, and that is the changing position of women in Asia and Africa.

The first aspect to be considered is that of the social effects of migration from the village to the city. Most dramatic in its obvious effects in Africa, there is a parallel development in Asia. Writing on the 'Anthropological Problems arising from Industrial Revolution' Professor Gluckman of Manchester University has this simple summary of what is involved in migration from the country to the town.

It seems to me apparent that the moment the African crosses his tribal boundary to go to the town, he is 'detribalized', out of the political control of the tribe. And in the town, the basic materials by which he lives are different: he walks on different ground, eats food at different hours and may be different food at that. He comes under different political authorities, and associates with different fellows. He works with different tools in a different system of organization.[9]

Life, in a word, is *different*, very different. Having regard to the very close-knit character of tribal life in which political and economic factors, custom and religion are inextricably bound up with one another, this kind of change means a real disintegration, whose effect on those who experience it will often be catastrophic.

Consider only the fact that migration of labour, primarily designed to earn money for taxation, must involve abnormal

[9] Max Gluckman in *Social Change in Modern Africa*, ed. by Aidan Southall (Oxford University Press, 1961), p. 69.

sex ratios, thereby profoundly affecting the family structure. In recent years the need for a stable labour force has led management to encourage labourers to bring their families with them and some provision has been made by the way of housing to make this possible. But this has been a late development. A vast unsettlement of African tribal society has long since taken place.

Furthermore, we must recognize that urban life is a threat to the security of the African family because both the man and his wife are removed from the disciplines and restraints of tribal life which, at least in the realm of sexual ethics, have a powerful influence. The African woman in an urban setting must necessarily lose the influence which she derived from the tribal rôles, agricultural and domestic, which cannot be performed in the town. And, as one writer has well observed, the very high status goal given to grandmotherhood in both Asia and Africa, which is some considerable compensation for all the troubles of life in a polygamous household, is likely to be out of reach because the children may scatter and the woman herself may retire to the country before it can be attained.[10]

The second aspect of social change to which reference has already been made in another context is the transition from a society in which status determined the life of the individual to one in which the individual has at least a measure of freedom to determine his own life by contract.

It is true, of course, that freedom to make a contract may be the last act which turns a freeman into a wage-slave. Yet a man whose relationships with other men are based on contract is a different kind of man from one whose position in life is determined solely by status. Contract provides, in however small a degree, a kind of opportunity which is not available in a custom-dominated society. The kind of freedoms based on a society where contractual relationships obtain are distinctively

[10] See Aidan Southall, *op. cit.*, p. 22.

western in character. Here, as much as anywhere, the breach between the old and the new is decisive.

Perhaps it may be noticed in passing that the distinctive freedom of western society resulting from its contractual nature is that it puts a premium upon the individual's exercise of choice. At once we find ourselves caught up in the far-reaching debate about the Christian approach in evangelism. Is the missionary to aim at individual decisions or corporate decisions? There is no easy answer. What appears to be certain is that one result of the impact of westernization on social life in Asia and Africa will be an increasing opportunity in certain segments of society to pursue the aim of individual conversion. This may be true even as we recognize that modern industrialization increasingly presents us with new forms of collective mentality which, in their openness to the appeal for conversion, are about as resistant as the ancient religious cultures of Asia and Africa.

Closely related in more ways than one to this transition from status to contract, as a basis for social organization, is the impact of westernization on the whole idea of the tribe as a political-economic-social and religious unit.

Here we must be clear that tribalism in Africa, like caste in India, is still immensely strong as a cohesive force resistant to westernization, and at heart is deeply opposed to modernization at anything but a very superficial level. What can be said, however, is that the sheer pressure of events, the inherent logic of the world's economic development, and the working of that technology which can alone deal with poverty, all these are working inexorably against the institutions and attitudes of mind which have traditionally gone with the tribe and with caste.

And, in so far as the tribe and the caste system are inadequate to meet the needs of modern society, so in the long-run the kinship group, which is the tribe writ small, will have to make way for the nuclear family in the western pattern. This may be expected to happen if Asia and Africa are to be successful in providing that 'middle class' which has so largely contributed to that very phenomenon we are considering—the western way of life. For it has been upon the basis of bourgeois, middle-class virtues, the belief in the gospel of work, of thrift and of self-discipline, that resources necessary to achieve the western world's technological civilizations have been built up. The great debate of our time, which divides our world, is whether the 'Western way' or the 'Communist way' of building a new world involves the least suffering for the majority of mankind.

But whichever 'way' emerges triumphant, there will be no room left either for the tribe or for caste.

The changing position of women in Asia and Africa is that fourth aspect of social change to which reference has been made. In this connection there is a subject to which very little attention has been paid and which provides in itself an important field for research. We have already considered woman in her capacity as wife and mother, as the mainstay of a family pattern which is disintegrating. We must also consider woman in herself as an individual in her own right, without regard to her function as wife and mother.

In this respect the significance of the role played by single-women missionaries can scarcely be exaggerated. For, as teachers or nurses, as doctors or pastoral workers, whether habited after the fashion of a religious order or undistinguished from other women by dress, these missionary women have been the agents of perhaps the most far-reaching change of all these that we have been considering.

That claim is not made simply by virtue of their immediate influence on one half of the human race. Rather it is that they have presented Asia and Africa with the actual demonstration that marriage and child-bearing is not the only vocation open to the ordinary woman. In doing this they have at the same time, though incidentally, greatly added to the dignity of marriage, because for the woman marriage becomes a vocation she can choose precisely because she has an alternative choice. Sociologically speaking it is, I believe, very difficult to overestimate the contribution made to the full understanding of Christian marriage by those women who, from free choice, have foregone that particular vocation.

In this idea of a woman having a vocation to remain single and *yet to live in the world and serve it*, the missionary movement has made a quite unique contribution to social change. The nuns of Buddhism and the occasional woman mystic in Islam are hardly exceptions.

One small, but immediate and very practical result of this missionary influence has been the slow but steady raising of the age of marriage for girls in Asia and Africa. Teaching and nursing became at once possibilities for Asian and African girls, even if only for a temporary period. For before their eyes and the eyes of their people were unmarried woman discharging precisely these responsibilities. Here is one of the most constructive of the impacts of the West upon Asia and Africa, even if its consequences are also revolutionary.

The Impact of Christianity

There remains for final consideration the disintegrating impact of the Christian religion, which as we have already seen, has been from the first an integral part of westernization. Precisely because Christianity has never been presented *in vacuo* but always in some relation to the culture of the person who did the presenting, it is difficult to specify any particular factor which was disintegrating solely by virtue of its Christian character. Perhaps it would be more accurate to see the Christian religion as one of those elements in a generally disintegrating impact which was always, in its essence, designed to be constructive. If something had to be destroyed, it was not in the sense of 'making a desert and calling it peace', but rather as a necessary act of demolition by way of preparation for a new building.

If the general impact of the West created a widely diffused 'uneasiness of mind', a feeling that the foundations were being shaken, Christianity, when presented not only as a truth to be accepted but as a certain kind of life to be lived, did generate a certain 'divine discontent' with things as they were.

Now the great medium of this 'divine discontent' was, beyond question, education, education as the West understood it, and what tended to be education in a European language. This in turn meant the opening of minds to the influence of Christian literature, and in the first instance this meant the Bible.

Immediately we see that Christianity meant an enormous widening of the mental horizon of those who submitted themselves to western education. And, as a matter of history, for the greater part of the nineteenth century Christian Missions had a predominant role to play in such education in India and China, and, down to the second World War, something very like a monopoly of it in tropical Africa. It was no accident that enquirers for Christian baptism in Uganda were universally known as 'readers'.

And the fact that the Bible was so staple a product of their reading meant that minds soaked in the Bible developed an historical perspective and a sense of purpose in historical development. Now both in India and in Africa, though for different reasons, history was a closed book. For the Hindu, history was of no account, for the things with which history are concerned are essentially illusory. They are without significant value themselves. For the African there were only tribal traditions disappearing into the mists of the past, because there were no written languages. But if history is to be taken seriously, and the Bible suggests that it is, then purpose begins to have a meaning, and the future is something men can make and not only endure.

All this meant a great widening of the mental horizon and a new world-view. Again, what a European language, European literature, and the Bible in particular revealed was manifestly inconsistent with much that was current thinking and practice, whether in Asian or African societies. This led many to a 'divine discontent'. Not all such, and in India no more than a very few, allowed this 'divine discontent' to bring them to accept the Christian Faith. But it did make them very critical of their own religion and culture. The significance of the Christian missionary movement is not solely to be gauged by the number of baptized Christians. Some of its most striking effects are to be seen in the radical changes which the great ethnic religions have been compelled to make in the image which they present to the world. Judged by the time span of the jet-age, the progress of Christianity in Asia and Africa may be dismissed as very slow, and its impact as very slight. This is the fashionable current view. But the catalytic effect of Christianity can only be judged by seeing how far-reaching have been the attempts of the other religions to reform themselves, and reinterpret their own fundamental principles, in the light of Christianity.

When Gandhi was assassinated because of his tremendous devotion to the cause of reconciliation between Hindus and Muslims, there was one common and universal reaction of Indian opinion. In that hour of darkness in their national life Indians of all persuasions interpreted the death of Gandhi in the light of the Crucifixion of Jesus Christ. It is easy to dismiss this as of small moment because it has not yet led those who made the comparison to go further and become disciples. But it does reveal a movement of the mind, a certain direction which is the direct fruit of the modern missionary movement.

Or again one may cite the missionary programmes of the reformed Hinduism, represented by the Ramakrisha Mission or the reformed Islam of the Ahmadiyyah sect, and note the almost slavish fidelity with which they have adopted all the missionary methods and techniques of the Christian movement. And the message they proclaim most certainly is not traditional Hinduism or traditional Islam.

So far disintegration has produced reformation rather than conversion. That is quite true, but we have not yet come to the end of the story. We may well repudiate the facile remark of Lord Cromer that 'Islam reformed is Islam no longer'. But we may reasonably ask whether Islam, or Hinduism or Buddhism, in so far as they have been reformed, have the inner reserves with which to meet the disintegrating impact of westernization. Time will show. In the next chapter an attempt will be made to do justice to what is happening today in these other great religions of mankind. What we must not fail to note is that Christianity has been a very effective challenger to these religions. It could be claimed that Christianity, as by no means the least significant aspect of westernization, has played a decisive part in disintegrating their old world-view.

There was an eventful day in 1830. July 13th was the day and Calcutta was the place. A young Scots missionary, Alexander Duff, had made friends with an Indian, Ram Mohun Roy, a brilliant scholar who, having rejected Hinduism, and found the Qur'an unsatisfactory, had found in the Bible what he felt to be an unparalleled source of moral and religious guidance. He was not a Christian, and he never became one, but he had a profound reverence for Jesus Christ, and a deep regard for Alexander Duff as one of Christ's disciples.

With Ram Mohun Roy's help, Duff had gathered round him a small group of boys who had begun to read English. At last the day came, July 13, 1830, when premises had been secured to start a school specializing in the teaching of English. Ram

G

Mohun Roy had already declared that the best short prayer for starting a school day was the Lord's Prayer. Alexander Duff opened proceedings by praying the Lord's Prayer slowly in Bengali. Then he put a copy of the Gospels into the hands of one of the boys and told him to read. This immediately led to the outcry that reading the Bible would make the boy a Christian. Ram Mohun Roy rallied them with the remark that he had read the Qur'an and it had not made him a Muslim! In this fashion the school started. In due course a number of the boys were, in fact, converted and baptized. But that is nothing like as significant as the fact that what Duff had started was a study of the English language and the reading of the Bible.

Windows were opened that day which have never been shut. And if it is pointed out that one sequel to Christian education has been the disintegration of the British Empire in India and Africa, we may without apology accept the impeachment.

They must be free

. . . who speak the tongue
That Shakespeare spake; the faith and morals hold
Which Milton held. . . .

You cannot preach the Christian Gospel without disintegrating all kinds of traditional bondage and so, in all kinds of unsuspected ways, make men and women thirsty for the freedom with which Christ makes men free, whether they recognize Christ or not. Once in history Christianity was married to the Greek language, the *lingua franca* of that age, and thereby disintegrated the old world in preparation for a new one. Something which can bear comparison with what happened then happened between 1830 and 1930, and the results of that later marriage may well carry the world through a new dark age to a brighter dawn, as also happened once before.

Of the disintegrating impact of westernization there can be

no doubt—*si monumentum requiris circumspice*. But it has all the while carried within it the seeds of reintegration, of the making of a new world order. Perhaps the question we have most seriously to address to ourselves is whether Christianity today is as effectively a part of the process of westernization as it was in the nineteenth and the first part of the twentieth century.

5

THE RESURGENT RELIGIONS
OF ASIA AND AFRICA

HENDRIK KRAEMER, the *doyen* of contemporary thinkers about the Christian Mission, has said:

For the first time since the Constantine victory in A.D. 312 and its consequences, the Christian Church is heading towards a real and spiritual encounter with the great non-Christian religions. Not only because the so-called younger churches, the fruit of the work of modern missions, live in the midst of them, but also because the fast growing interdependence of the whole world forces the existence and vitality of these religions upon us, and makes them a challenge to the Church to manifest in new terms its spiritual and intellectual integrity and value.[1]

We are living, that is to say, in a world which, religiously speaking, is a pluralistic society. We are confronted, as western Christians have not for the most part been consciously confronted before, with the theological problems of co-existence. We may go further and say that theologians of the West will need more and more to take into consideration the contribution of the great ethnic religions of the world to Christian theology itself. Familiar as we are with the fact that in one way and another Zoroastrianism, the mystery religions, and the whole Greek view of life materially influenced the development of Christian theology, we are less familiar with the idea that what Dr Kraemer calls 'a real and spiritual encounter with

---

[1] Hendrik Kraemer, *Religion and the Christian Faith* (Lutterworth Press, 1956), p. 20.

the great non-Christian religions' needs in our day minds as
flexible as those of the great Alexandrian school, and a new
Christian apologetic.

Perhaps, at this point, it may be suggested that the convenient short-hand term 'non-Christian religions', even though
used by Dr Kraemer, should be discarded. Hinduism, Islam,
Buddhism, the African's traditional expression of his own
spiritual awareness, these are not to be understood negatively
as simply being 'non-Christian', to be judged and dismissed
for their difference from the Christian Faith; but rather to be
understood first of all for what they are, for the revelation
they offer of what man is and how man thinks, above all for
the testimony they bear to the continuous working of the
Holy Spirit of God at all times and in all places. An Indian
Christian speaks with authority when he says,

> Modern Christian theology should not persist in ignoring the
> fact that the history of religions continues after Christ, and in
> addition to the history of the Christian Church. The history of
> salvation is realized not only in the confines of the organized
> Churches but also in the total scope of the history of religions.[2]

To endorse that judgment is in no way whatever to belittle
the uniqueness of Christ, to doubt that the *fulness* of salvation
is to be found in Christ alone. Endorsement of that judgment
is only another way of affirming that Christ is the Lord of
history, of all history.

A further comment on Dr Kraemer's statement may serve to
start us on our exploration of the resurgent religions of Asia
and Africa. There is one significant difference between the
Christian encounter with the other religions today and the
encounter at the time of Constantine. The difference can be
summarized in some graphic words of Dr Edwin Hatch, in his

[2] *Religion and Society*, ed. P. D. Devanandan and M. M. Thomas, vol. viii,
No. 4, December 1961, p. 4.

Hibbert Lectures for 1888 on *The Influence of Greek Ideas and Usages upon the Christian Church.* Dr Hatch was describing the difficulty of recapturing the actual viewpoint of those ancient writers whose opinions are known only from the extracts quoted by their opponents. And in particular he referred to the difficulty of assessing accurately the character of the opposition which was overcome by the post-Constantine Church. He wrote: 'When the associated Christian communities won at length their hard-fought battle, they burned the enemy's camp'.[3]

How different is the situation with regard to our subject! This new encounter in which we are involved is very fully documented, embarrassingly so. The battle, if we be allowed to continue the metaphor, is being hard-fought and is not within sight of being won!

Indeed, the very term 'resurgence' in relation to the other religions of the world may not improperly be held to signify a 'counter-attack'. But a 'counter-attack', in so far as it is successful, leads into a new phase of action. Resurgence can well be a renaissance and may, in some cases, properly denote a revival of religion. We shall find evidence of this in due course. But first we can best study the resurgence in terms of a 'counter-attack'. This counter-attack has been varied in its nature. In India, for instance, it has been directed against the challenge of Christianity, and to a lesser degree, at least at first, against western domination. In the Middle East, to a far greater extent, it has been a counter-attack against western imperialism and only gradually has come to be explicitly an answer to Christianity. In Japan and Africa the word 'counter-attack' is too strong. The resurgence is to be understood more as a spontaneous response to the traumatic experience of seeing a traditional pattern of life totally overthrown.

It is of some importance for our perspective to realize that

[3] Edwin Hatch, *op. cit.* (Williams & Norgate, 1891), p. 10.

the great expansion of Christianity during the nineteenth century was materially aided by two factors. On the one hand it coincided with a period during which spiritual decay, a loss of any real depth of faith, seemed to be the common experience of most religions. On the other hand it coincided with the enormous expansion of western power based on western expertise in the application of scientific knowledge. Christianity extended its influence as one aspect of westernization. The suggestion may also be advanced that in the so-called Christian world there had also been a decay of spiritual life comparable to that of the other religious cultures. If this be allowed, then the eighteenth and early nineteenth century revivals within the Christian Church anticipated the revivals in the other religions. How far any of these revivals, Christian or otherwise, signify anything approaching a return to the Ages of Faith, may well be doubted. Here, perhaps, we may recognize the inwardness of the distinctively religious dilemma of our time, and find a clue to the ideology which has promoted the concept of a Parliament of Religions, and which makes the philosophy of Dr Radhakrishnan so widely accepted in the West as well as in India.

However that may be, and I have only hinted at an explanation which calls for a great deal of study, we shall be right if we take as a clue to every aspect of the resurgence of the other religions the fact that this resurgence was, in one form or another, a response to the impact of the West.

Hinduism

Turning first to India, the resurgence of Hinduism was, a direct result of the Christian missionary movement, acting either directly in India itself or indirectly through the influence of public opinion in England being brought to bear on the East India Company and the House of Commons.

Dr Kenneth Ingham opens his book *Reformers in India 1793-1833* with the following paragraph:

The growth of Indian nationalism has tended to obscure the contribution of external forces to the development of India. In the field of social progress emphasis has been placed upon the activities of the Brahma Samaj, the Arya Samaj, and more recently the Congress Party, rather than upon the work of Europeans in India. But the history of the Christian missionary achievement is older than any of these indigenous movements, and prepared the way for them, to a degree far greater than the number of Christians in India might now suggest. Conversions to Christianity were proportionately few, but the influence of missionaries upon social conditions was outstanding.[4]

That judgment is significantly endorsed by an enthusiastic modern apologist for Hinduism, D. S. Sarma, from whose important book *The Renaissance of Hinduism* much that follows will be a direct or indirect quotation.

There were new forces working silently towards a great Renaissance which came into full vigour in the early years of the present century. The most important of these forces is, of course, the spread of English education which broke the intellectual isolation of the Indian mind and brought it into contact with Western science, literature and history. The result of this was a great mental expansion similar to that which the European nations experienced at the time of the Revival of Classical Learning in the fifteenth and sixteenth centuries . . . In the light of this new knowledge many an evil custom in Hindu society, hitherto regarded as a decree of God, appeared in its true colours as the folly of man. Sati, infanticide, enforced widowhood, child marriages, untouchability, purdah, devadasi, the caste system and prohibition of foreign travel began to lose their tyrannical hold on the minds of Hindus. And reformers arose who were determined to purge the society of these evils.

Along with the new knowledge came the fierce attacks of the early Christian Missions on Hinduism and Hindu society. The zealous missionaries who never failed to point their finger of

[4] Kenneth Ingham, *op. cit.* (Cambridge University Press, 1956), p. 1.

scorn at our religious and social institutions were educators as well as crusaders. They opened schools and colleges where they not only imparted the new secular knowledge, but also taught Christianity as the only true religion. These two forces acting in combination produced in the minds of the educated classes for a time either a thoroughgoing scepticism or a partial leaning towards Christianity, but ultimately they served only to arouse Hinduism from its sleep.[5]

That is a very important statement by a thoughtful and convinced Hindu. Consider his phrases, 'the fierce attacks of the early Christian Missions' and 'their finger of scorn at our religious and social institution'. Those phrases are fully justified. It is perhaps, in some degree, the measure of the achievement of those early missionaries that missionaries in India today do not need to make 'such fierce attacks' or 'to point the finger of scorn'. A sense of perspective is called for in passing judgment on the past. Dr Ingham makes a valuable observation when, looking back and considering the attacks of those early missionaries on the caste system in India, he says:

They might easily have been driven to accept the general view of Englishmen in India, that caste was merely the equivalent of the European social order, conservative indeed, but only as befitted a predominantly agricultural and under-developed community. Had they brought to the problem a spirit of curious interest in a strange phenomenon instead of a burning faith in the transcendental nature of their own religion, they might indeed have reached that conclusion; they might also have become better Oriental scholars, but they would have contributed less to social reform.[6]

It is no use being squeamish about history. The important thing is to understand it. An introduction to understanding how Hinduism appeared to a learned English traveller at the beginning the nineteenth century can be seen in the vividly

[5] D. S. Sarma, *op. cit.* (Benares Hindu University, 1944), pp. 68-69.
[6] Kenneth Ingham, *op. cit.*, p. 21.

written chapters of *Christian Researches in Asia*, by Claudius Buchanan, of which it has been said that its publication in 1811 'aroused probably the greatest interest in Indian affairs that had ever been felt in England'.[7] Anyone who has read this horrifying description of the worship of Juggernaut and the human sacrifices involved, as well as of the burning of widows, and infanticide, will not be surprised as the exhortation of Archdeacon T. F. Middleton, soon to be the first Anglican bishop in India, which he addressed to an S.P.C.K. Missionary, the Rev. C. A. Jacobi, at a Meeting held on March 23, 1813, to bid him farewell. The Archdeacon said:

Amidst all the darkness which still envelopes the Heathen World, the superstitions of Hindooism are calculated to excite, in a peculiar degree, emotions of pity and horror. Very far removed from a state of barbarism, retaining even the vestiges of ancient science and refinement, gifted with faculties which culture might elevate to the proudest eminence of intellectual attainment, mild in their nature, and humane in their deportment, the Hindoos present the most lamentable spectacle of religious depravation, and serve to demonstrate how weak and wretched is human nature in its most favoured circumstances, unblessed with a knowledge of the true God and His reasonable service.[8]

Horror and pity, those two quite genuine emotions, were the driving force which enabled religious opinion in England to prevail over the reluctance of the East India Company and of the British Government to take action in passing the legislation without which there would have been no social reform.

A petition presented to Parliament by William Wilberforce in the House of Commons, and Lord Gambier in the House of Lords on behalf of the Committee of the Church Missionary Society, faithfully reflects the mood of the time, both in regard to horror and pity, and also something more, a spirit of res-

[7] Kenneth Ingham, *op. cit.*, p. 35.   [8] *Missionary Register*, 1814, p. 12.

ponsibility which was never wholly lacking, even in the midst of 'fierce attacks' and the pointing of fingers of scorn. In this petition the following passages are relevant:

That your Petitioners, believing the nations of India, both Mohammedan and Hindu, to be in a state of mental and moral degradation, which may reasonably excite the warmest zeal for the introduction of the Gospel among them, and esteeming their condition, as fellow subjects of the British Crown, to be an additional motive to this important work, have considered it to be one great purpose of this institution, to provide missionaries and other means of instruction for our Indian settlements and adjacent countries . . . That, far from wishing the authority of Government to be employed in imposing Christianity on the Mohammedans and Hindoos, your Petitioners would deprecate any departure from the principles of toleration towards the professors of those religions: but they earnestly desire to promote the peaceable diffusion of moral and religious light, by all prudent and quick means. . . .[9]

Further evidence of the spirit of responsibility which marched with 'horror and pity' is to be seen in the recognition from the very outset of the modern missionary movement that there must be serious study of the other great religions, and that the best scholarship must be devoted to it. A good illustration of this is to be found in the researches of William Carey. In support of the campaign to secure the prohibition of sati, the burning of widows on their husbands' funeral pyres, he collected from the pandits the evidence of the *Sastras*, the ancient Hindu writings, and in this way confirmed the conviction of the missionaries 'that the self-immolation of widows, though countenanced by Hindu law, was in no way commanded by it'.[10]

Carey's scholarly researches in this matter anticipated by

[9] *Missionary Register*, 1813, pp. 121-123.
[10] Kenneth Ingham, *op. cit.*, p. 45.

fourteen years the same conclusions which Ram Mohun Roy,
the founder of the Brahma Samaj, published in 1818.

The importance of that illustration is that it points us to
one crucially important development in the Hindu renaissance
—the restoration of religious self-respect to Hinduism by a
rediscovery of its own most ancient religious traditions.
Western scholarship, Christian scholarship, as well as Christian protest, was the main external stimulus toward this
recovery of self-respect. No small part of the resurgence of the
religions of Asia and Africa consists precisely in this new self-
awareness.

D. S. Sarma pays an interesting testimony to this by showing
how Ram Mohun Roy, who was at first hostile to the exten-
sion of British Rule in India, later changed his mind. Sarma
says that

closer contact with Englishmen and their literature made him
believe that it was nothing short of a divine dispensation that
India had at last come under the rule of 'a nation who not only
are blessed with the enjoyment of civil and political liberty but
also interest themselves in promoting liberty and social happiness
as well as free inquiry into literary and religious subjects among
those nations to which their influence extends.'[11]

That tribute by a devout Hindu, quoting another Hindu,
strikes a note which has never been wholly lost in the renaissance of Hinduism, and goes far to explain the relations
of Britain with independent India.

Ram Mohun Roy's leaning towards Christianity, though he
never became a Christian, and the increasing nationalism of
his followers, provoked a conservative reaction. The Arya
Samaj, founded by Swami Dayananda, while accepting the
social programme of the Brahma Samaj, insisted on finding
the inspiration for their reforms in devotion to the ancient

[11] D. S. Sarma, *op. cit.*, p. 87.

classics of Hinduism. For the Arya Samajists, the West had done its work of stimulating Hinduism, and from now on Hinduism could carry on the task itself without further help from the West.

Here we find the second strain in the resurgence of Hinduism. The restoration of self-respect is followed by a reassertion of value, a reassertion which, under successive spiritual leaders like Shri Ramakrishna Paramhansa, Swami Vivekananda, Rabindrinath Tagore, Mahatma Gandhi, and Dr Radhakrishnan has brought Hinduism out of its defeatism and made it, as it had never been before, a missionary religion in its own right.

Rhapsodizing about the teachings of Swami Vivekananda and the impact he made on the imagination of many in the West, D. S. Sarma illustrates this new claim when he writes:

Of all the religions of the world, it is Vedanta alone that can make men strong and self-reliant, having unbounded faith in themselves. By insisting on the inherent divinity of the human soul under all circumstances, it gives hope of infinite progress to every man, however degraded and fallen he may be.[12]

The logic of such a view must be the proclamation of such a gospel to others. In the conclusion of the book, Sarma arrives at just this point. He says:

Islam and Christianity will, no doubt, insist on their rights of propaganda and conversion. We cannot quarrel with them on that ground, so long as they do not employ force or unfair means to compass their object. We must, of course, claim the same rights and freely take into our fold not only all those who once belonged to it and want to come back to it, but also those who are born in other faiths, but want to embrace Hinduism. Hinduism has latterly been content to remain only an ethnic religion. But in future it should become a creedal religion also. . . .[13]

[12] D. S. Sarma, *op. cit.*, pp. 302-303.   [13] D. S. Sarma, *op. cit.*, p. 643.

There speaks the voice of resurgent Hinduism, as authentically part of the resurgence as is the universalism of the Ramakrishna mission and the philosophy of Dr Radhakrishnan which both, in their several ways, would woo the western mind to accept a religious 'neutralism' that sees all religions as equally authentic roads to the summit. No one can read the passionate utterances of a Swami Vivekananda or the cool reasoning of a Dr Radhakrishnan and not be deeply moved by their sincerity. Each in his own way offers to the world the fine flower of the best and highest Hindu thought. They illustrate as well as anything can do the fact that the renaissance of Hinduism is the renaissance of India.

Yet, when one has said that, believing it to be true, there is a stop in the mind. No study of the renaissance of Hinduism can ignore the influence of Mahatma Gandhi as one of the heroic personalities who did so much to establish India in the world's respect. It is well known that for all his devotion to the Sermon on the Mount, his real spiritual home was in the Vedas. As much as being a symbol of the renaissance of India he is a symbol of the resurgence of Hinduism. Central to any understanding of Mahatma Gandhi is an understanding of his revulsion against the impact of the West. Sarma thus describes him on his return from South Africa:

He declared that he was a determined opponent of modern European civilization, as it was based on violence, greed and competition and was materialistic in character. He believed that the ancient civilization of India was superior to modern European civilization, because it was based on non-violence, contentment and co-operation, and was spiritual in character. Therefore, the advancing tide of Western civilization should be stemmed at all costs—we should be strictly Swadeshi—Swadeshi in religion, Swadeshi in politics and Swadeshi in economics.[14]

[14] D. S. Sarma, *op. cit.*, pp. 472-473. Maurice Zinkin in *Development for Free Asia*, pp. 11-112, presents a balancing picture of the contribution of Mahatma Gandhi to India's economic development.

It is a fact of history that India, under Pandit Jawaharlal Nehru, diverged further and further away from this Gandhian ideal. Some of the most conscientious minds in India were not content with having re-established the values of India's ancient religious tradition, and with having a number of great thinkers and spiritual leaders who commanded the respect of all mankind. They were overwhelmed with the appalling poverty of the masses of India's people. They were convinced that the first priority in India's thought and action now must be economic development. And this meant a frank acceptance of that westernization, at least in economic affairs, which Gandhi had tried to resist.

Among the more percipient of modern studies of the Asian scene is Maurice Zinkin's book *Development for Free Asia*, the larger part of which is devoted to India. In his second chapter he writes of 'The Price of Development'. For all its brevity, the chapter is a brilliant and sensitive exposition of the fact that economic development depends upon certain basic assumptions in the field of ideas, assumptions largely alien to the traditional thought of the East. One of these basic assumptions is the need to want development harder than anything else, to allow nothing to stand in its way. Such, in practice, is the outcome of the spirit of enquiry about the nature of the world, which is in turn based on the conviction that the world is good and has a real value in itself—an insight common to both the Greek and Hebrew view of life, and the root cause of the technological development of the West. Maurice Zinkin ends this chapter with a paragraph which ought to be disturbing:

Europe has changed its values since the Middle Ages. It produces fewer saints, perhaps also fewer artists, than in the Middle Ages; but the material well-being of its people, their control over their physical environment, is going up at a rate inconceivable to their mediaeval ancestors. What Europe has done Asia can do, has indeed already begun to do—in Japan rather more than begun. But there will be a loss. When in India the income per head reaches that of the United States today, it may no longer produce saints like Vinoba Bhave. The world will be poorer as well as richer.[15]

A question is there posed which faces all the religions of mankind, Christianity no less than the others. Can a religion be radically *this-world*-affirming without the *other-world*-denying? Can we welcome material development without spiritual impoverishment? Can we develop an asceticism which says 'no' for the right reasons and not for the wrong ones? Can we discover an ethic for the affluent society? In a word, can a religious faith be the inspiring heart of the world that is coming to be? Anyone who imagines there is an easy answer to that question has not begun to think. At this point every resurgent religion, every sign of revival in any religion, stands under a huge question mark.

Islam

In this chapter attention has been concentrated upon India and Hinduism because in India the resurgence of Hinduism has been more unambiguously a religious movement than perhaps anywhere else. In this respect there is a considerable contrast with the Middle East, and with those other areas whose religious culture has been fashioned by Islam.

In our period Islam as a political idea was under a far more dangerous threat from the West than that which had confronted it even in the time of the Crusaders. The Ottoman Empire to which the political hopes of Islam had been tied was under pressure by the western powers and was beginning to disintegrate. Islam as a religious idea seemed to lack any dynamic force. The need for inner revival was the starting point in the thought of those Muslim thinkers who heralded

[15] Maurice Zinkin, *op. cit.*, p. 7.

the Arab awakening, created Arab Nationalism, tried to recon-
cile it with the pan-Islamic ideal, and sought to revive the
glorious first age of Islam. How, in a word, were Muslims to
bridge the gap between what Islamic society should be and
what it had become?

Like the cry in Hinduism, 'back to the Vedas', there was a
corresponding effort to point Muslims back to Mohammed
with the insistence that the Qur'an properly understood could
meet the challenge of the West. But to a degree which was
never the same in India, and could not be, geography had
bound the Middle East with western Europe. The appeal of
western thought, and the spectacle of western technological
achievement, pressed much more intimately upon the peoples
of Islam in the Middle East and North Africa than it ever
did in India.

This meant that from the first the question which really
dominated the minds of Muslims, men like Jamal al-Din al-
Afghani, Muhammad Abduh, Rashid Rida, Taha Husayn,
and many others was the problem of how to accept western
civilization without abandoning Islam. Before we consider
the measure of their success, it is important to realize that
these were men of prophetic calibre, personalities of great
dynamism and appeal, who proclaimed with passion their
belief in Islam and kindled a real pride in the fact of being
Muslim. Their great hope lay in recovering for Muslims a
real sense of the worth and value of their community, the
Dar-ul-Islam. In this they were beyond question successful.

But the process by which they made their achievement must
raise a serious doubt as to whether the resurgence of Islam,
as it took place and is still taking place, can be said to be a
religious revival. Raising that question points to the need for
a great deal of patient and sympathetic research into what is
happening in the Muslim world today. There is plenty of
evidence of traditional orthodoxy being as strong and fanati-

H

cal as ever. There is a wealth of simple piety among ordinary Muslims.[16] There are vigorous heretical movements which are enthusiastically missionary, such as the Ahmadiyyah movement and the Ismai'ilis. But none of these answers the question as to whether there is a religious revival of Islam as a faith. For as we have seen earlier, the questions being posed by the modern world are essentially a challenge to religious faith.

At an early stage in the nineteenth century the argument was being advanced that

> The progress of Europe . . . is not in any sense due to its being Christian. Christianity is a religion which aims at happiness in the next world, not in this . . . Thus if the Muslim countries try to adopt the causes of European progress they will not be adopting Cristianity.[17]

This has been a widely held view, and it was even stated that 'to adopt European institutions is really to fulfil the spirit and purpose of the *Shari'a*.[18] It is illuminating to see where such an opinion led. Following that insight, another thinker, Quasim Amin, wrote a book urging the emancipation of women. This produced so violent a storm of reaction from the conservatives that, in Amin's case, it looked as if the Islamic scaffolding of his thought had collapsed. From then on he stressed, as the only standards of judgment, 'freedom, progress and civilization' and went on record as saying that 'it is useless to hope to adopt the sciences of Europe without coming within the radius of its moral principles; the two things are indissolubly connected, and we must therefore be prepared for change in every aspect of our life.'[19]

---

[16] See the impressive evidence collected by Constance E. Padwick in *Muslim Devotions: A study of Prayer Manuals in Common Use* (SPCK, 1961).

[17] Albert Hourani, *Arabic Thought in the Liberal Age, 1789-1939* (Oxford University Press, 1962), p. 91.

[18] Albert Hourani, *op. cit.*, p. 92.   [19] Albert Hourani, *op. cit.*, p. 169.

It is difficult not to see in the development of Muslim thinking in the second half of the nineteenth century and in the
twentieth century that 'the centre of attention is no longer
Islam as a religion, it is rather Islam as a civilization.'[20] Let
us be clear that an orthodox Muslim would not easily accept
that there is a real distinction. Islam for him is a Faith and
a Society and a Way of living. It is all of these at the same time
and all the time. But, in so far as this integration is controlled
by the Faith, as represented by the Qur'an and the traditions of
the first four Caliphs, there is a very uneasy alliance with a
technological civilization. It is to some extent the uneasiness
of this alliance which justifies the statement that, in practice,
the emphasis tends to be on the civilization and not the Faith,
and that for the very practical reason that 'Islamic' civilization,
which is fundamentally a way of life controlled by the Arabic
language and Arabic thought, is a unifying factor, whereas
the Faith is divisive.

This, I suggest, is the inner secret of the preoccupation of
the leaders of the Muslim world with the problems of unity,
and, where the unity of the Muslim world as a whole has
been unobtainable, then the unity of the nation.

And it is at this point that we can appraise the great significance for Islam that in the last twenty years almost the whole
world of Islam has become politically independent. This opens
up incalculable vistas of hope for Muslims. Indeed, political
independence is in the strictest sense the precondition for
Muslims being able to have a full Muslim life. It is only
now that we will be able to see whether in fact Islam as a
religion is really resurgent, or whether, as a religion, it will
retreat before the secularist temper of the age.

Islam's dilemma has been expressed very movingly by a
young Austrian Jew who, on his conversion to Islam, adopted
the name of Muhammad Asad. In his book *The Road to*

---

[20] Albert Hourani, *op. cit.*, p. 114.

Mecca he expresses something of his anxiety about his adopted home:

> Never before, I reflected, have the worlds of Islam and the West come so close to one another as to-day. This closeness is a struggle, visible and invisible. Under the impact of Western cultural influences, the souls of many Muslims, men and women, are slowly shrivelling. They are letting themselves be led away from their erstwhile belief that an improvement of living standards should be but a means to improving man's spiritual perceptions; they are falling into the same idolatry of 'progress' into which the Western world fell after it had reduced religion to a mere melodious tinkling somewhere in the background of happening; and are thereby growing smaller in stature, not greater: for all cultural imitation, opposed as it is to creativeness, is bound to make people small.[21]

Crisis Religion

I have chosen to illustrate the theme of this chapter by considering a few facets of those great religious cultures which are Hinduism and Islam. I have been concerned primarily to consider the dilemmas which confront these religions, and by implication, Christianity itself. In the space available it is quite impossible to do justice to these religions as great expressions of faith. For the same reason I have made no attempt to consider Buddhism or Judaism, though each in its own way has shown a development of a comparable kind to what we have seen in Hinduism and Islam.

There remains, however, to be noted a somewhat different form of religious experience. For lack of a more adequate term, I will call this 'crisis-religion'. And the most dramatic contemporary forms of this are to be found on the one hand in the New Religions of Japan as they have developed since 1945, and on the other hand in the syncretistic sects of Africa, with which may be associated the 'cargo' cults of the Pacific, and

[21] Muhammad Asad, *op. cit.* (Max Reinhardt, London, 1954), pp. 347-348.

the Peyote cult and similar prophetic movements among the Indians of North, Central and South America.

The crisis in the case of Japan was its overwhelming defeat in war, the discrediting of Shinto, the essentially Japanese expression of religion, and the de-divinization of the Emperor. Together these represented a psychic upheaval of the first magnitude. A vast spiritual vacuum was created and to fill this vacuum there has been the mushroom growth of new religions.

Essentially they are attempts to provide the Japanese people with a new basis for social harmony. The genius of Japan flowered in a harmonious ordering of society based on an intricate interplay of personal loyalties—loyalties within the family, within innumerable groupings clustered round some leader, within the corporate life of the nation focussed upon the Emperor. Otherwise than in respect of this last focus, the new religions of Japan are meeting the needs of the Japanese people. And a distinguished Japanese Christian thinker would insist that what is happening in Japan is 'essentially a religious revival'.[22]

But what that thinker says of one sect in particular, the Soka Gakkai, is substantially true of all these new religions. They are a response to a political, social and religious crisis.

Although the situation in Africa, the Pacific, and among the Indians of the Americas is very different from that in Japan, yet here also the essential character of all the innumerable indigenous manifestations of religion is that they are a response to a crisis. The crisis here is not defeat in war as in Japan, but a deeply felt defeat in the realm of the spirit. The security of the old traditional religious view-point has been shattered by the impact of an alien culture, bringing with it a new way of life to which the old religion could not adjust.

[22] Yoshimitsu Endo, *Soka Gakkai, The Study of a Society for the Creation of Value*, reprinted from the *Anglican Theological Review*, April 1964.

The African religious consciousness, for instance, and it may be held to represent the others, has not disappeared. It has gone underground. Repressed by its inadequacy to confront the Juggernaut of western power, it has erupted in forms as various as the philosophical concept of *négritude*; as the idea of an African personality, sponsored by many of the intellectual élite; as varieties of Pentecostal sects whose doctrinal orthodoxy, by Christian standards, is in some cases almost unimpeachable; as sects which in their syncretism tend to lose themselves in the old paganism; as a frank revival of witchcraft; each and all of these being in their varying ways attempts to find a new basis for security. Above all they are attempts to assert the self-respect of the African as a human being, a self-respect which the white man has affronted by his arrogant denial to the Africans of a self-hood which had a true dignity.

In these varied forms we have what may be called the crisis-religion of Africa. It should also be realized that it is a real element, just below the surface, in all the Christian churches of Africa. And it has a very close relationship with African nationalism. In this last respect the crisis-religions of Asia, Africa, the Pacific and the Americas have something in common with the resurgent religions with which this chapter has been mainly concerned. They all raise the question, to which we must now turn, as to whether, at this moment, nationalism is not man's 'other religion'—the religion which really commands his loyalty.

6

NATIONALISM, MAN'S OTHER RELIGION

No servant can be slave to two masters; for either he will hate the first and love the second, or he will be devoted to the first and think nothing of the second. You cannot serve God and Money.[1]

That is one of the most stark and uncompromising statements of the many such made by our Lord. It corresponds in its starkness with that epitome of the Old Testament revelation—'You shall do homage to the Lord your God and worship Him alone'.[2] The cry of the Muezzin is Islam's echo of the other two great monotheistic religions—'There is no God except God'. As the great Koranic Surah on the Unity of God, no. 112, has it:

He is God alone, God the eternal.
He does not beget and He is not begotten.
There is none co-equal with Him.

For Islam the unforgiveable is to associate anyone or anything with God. God and idolatry are incompatible. Such is the unequivocal testimony of monotheism whether Jewish, Christian or Islamic. We may press this further and say that when our Lord spoke of money as a rival deity he intended us to understand by that all that in any way claims our ultimate allegiance—property, family, nation. The great prophets of Israel spoke as plainly. Islam in its pristine flowering was as uncompromising.

[1] Matt. 6.24. NEB.　　[2] Matt. 4.10. NEB.

The other religions of mankind have been much less insistent upon the otherness, the uniqueness of God. They have stressed his immanence and in this way have lent themselves to an identification of religion and race which has hitherto, though today in a lessening degree, characterized Hinduism on the one hand and on the other the tribal religions of Africa.

But the fact we have to face, as we study nationalism, is that it would appear that those whose professed faith is monotheistic and those for whom the universe contains many points of reference all find it about equally easy, in given circumstances, to accept nationalism as their other religion or at the very least as a 'subordinate standard'.

By nationalism I mean that deep inner attitude of mind which distinguishes one group of people, large or small, calling for an exclusive loyalty, which in the last analysis limits humanity to that group, and which tends all too easily to treat inhumanly those outside that group. It is this idolatry of the group which we have to try to understand, for it is a clue to much that is happening in our world, and presents the Christian missionary enterprise with one of its greatest challenges. Yet this very idolatry of the group needs to have our sympathetic understanding, nor should that need argument for we do not stand outside this idolatry as curious spectators. None of us is really free to cast the first stone at another, when it comes to this particular form of idol worship. As we pursue our investigations we shall find much in the infra-structure of nationalism which is not only morally neutral but spiritually significant and important. This is what makes nationalism as a religion so ambiguous, makes us aware of how very easily we find ourselves having two religions at the same time, and before we know where we are, we are trying to do what our Lord categorically defined as impossible. It is for this reason that this chapter began as it did. For in our Lord's statement we have a canon of judgment by which we can distinguish between group loyalty and group idolatry.

A Japanese Religion

Let us consider first one of those 'crisis' religions already briefly noticed at the end of the last chapter—that new religion in Japan known as Soka Gakkai.

It is a sound principle that, when we deal with something as unfamiliar, and perhaps uncongenial, as the religious experience of another people, we should do so humbly, trying to feel with them and not to judge them. As we turn to look at this one of the new religions of Japan we may like to have in our minds the first verse of Cecil Spring-Rice's hymn:

I vow to thee, my country, all earthly things above,
Entire and whole and perfect, the service of my love:
The love that asks no question, the love that stands the test,
That lays upon the altar the dearest and the best;
The love that never falters, the love that pays the price,
The love that makes undaunted the final sacrifice.

Those words are a perfect expression of the faith of the Japanese Kamikaze suicide pilots, of the last war. One of these in his last letter home summarized this devotion in the couplet:

Like cherry blossoms
In the spring
Let us fall
Clear and radiant.

The Japanese Admiral who had been responsible for the policy of the suicide planes wrote this message to the Young People of Japan immediately before he committed *harakiri*:

You are the treasure of the nation. With all the fervour of spirit of the special attackers strive for the welfare of Japan and for peace throughout the world.

That last clause echoes the second verse of Spring-Rice's hymn. But in a moment of national crisis most hearts are moved by the first verse which I have quoted. And those of us who know ourselves to be most cowardly will be the last to gibe at any loyalty which can command 'the final sacrifice'. Here, indeed is something intrinsically noble to which we must offer the tribute of our respect, even when we must question the object should it ever come to assume the proportions of God.

Soka Gakkai is one response, perhaps the most vigorous and the most rapidly growing of all, to that Admiral's appeal to the young people of Japan. The roots of Soka Gakkai go back to the Buddhist monk Nichiren (1222-1282) whose life-span covered one of the most dramatic periods of Japanese history. During that time Japan was threatened with a Mongol invasion. It was this crisis which produced the message of Nichiren, the main characteristic of which was the identification of religion with the national life, claiming as he did that the two are one in health and disease. This, of course, tended towards a complete intolerance of all who did not accept the message, an intolerance which is a marked characteristic of Soka Gakkai today. 'If those who preach false doctrines are suppressed,' said Nichiren, 'and those who hold the true faith are respected, then there will be tranquility throughout the land, and the country will be at peace'[3]—a sentiment which history makes clear is by no means confined either to Japan or to periods of crisis.

Here we see nationalism as a religion without any qualification whatever, and a wholly this-worldly religion at that. The formidable fact which has to be noticed is that this religion, with its fanatical intolerance of all other religions, claims to

[3] From *Rissho Ankoko Ron*, an essay by Nichiren quoted by Harry Thomsen in *The New Religions of Japan* (Charles Tuttle Co., Rutland, Vermont, U.S.A. and Tokyo), p. 95.

be an expression of Buddhism. Something of the same quality is to be found in Sinhalese Buddhism in Ceylon today. Here we see graphically how nationalism as a religion can appear to be completely compatible with another religion whose fundamental premises it denies. Having regard to a great deal in the record of the Christian Church we will be slow to pass an easy judgment of condemnation. We must go a great deal deeper still if we are to understand the forces which go to the creation of nationalism, and so easily impel it to become a religion.

Nationalism in Africa

In the last chapter we saw Africa as an area where some of the manifestations of religion can fairly be given the title 'crisis' though in a quite different sense from the use of that term to describe what we have seen in Japan. The African picture is vastly more complicated, and generalizations in regard to Africa must be accepted with caution.

The deep under-swell of African life today is a determined revolt against everything and everyone who treats Africa and things African as being inferior. There is in Africa a widespread mood of self-assertion, which, however bizarre may be some of the forms it takes, however annoying and indeed sometimes painful to the white man, is in its essence a forceful assertion of the dignity of the individual African. The African has been pushed around long enough. Now, if anyone is going to do the pushing around, it will be the African. Europeans who resent being pushed around have curiously short memories! The African has a race memory going back for centuries.

What is important for us to realize, however, is that this revolt of the African is not only negative in character. There is deep resentment in it. There is an increasing element of race-hatred against the white world in it. But there are also positive elements in it which need to be understood, and in so far as they are both appreciated and taken seriously many mitigate the more negative elements. One of these positive elements is an awareness of the African past. For a very long time it was assumed that the African had no past which preceded the coming of the white man. Today paleontologists and anthropologists and prehistorians have established that Africa is at any rate one of the original nurseries of the human race. Historians have demonstrated that Africa has produced both cultures and political systems which are not to be despised. Sociologists have given a new value to complex patterns of family life. Meanwhile the observer of the contemporary scene can point to a large number of Africans of the highest ability who have in one generation moved from a family in which illiteracy was the rule to positions of great responsibility which they have responsibly taken. With so many men and women of such calibre already reshaping Africa, who is to put limits to what Africa can become?

Side by side with this sense of Africa's past, there is a new discovery of what we may call 'Africanness', a word more happily expressed in the French word *négritude*, coined by the philosopher-poet and statesman, Léopold Senghor of Senegal. He has himself defined this as 'the whole complex of civilized values—cultural, economic, social and political—which characterize the black people, or more precisely the Negro-African world.' And he goes on to say: 'The sense of communion, the gift of mythmaking, the gift of rhythm, such are the essential elements of *négritude*, which you will find indelibly stamped on all the works and activities of the black man.'

All this he develops to show its outworking in what he calls a 'community-based' society:

in which the hierarchy—and therefore spiritual power—is founded on spiritual and democratic values: on the law of primogeniture and election, in which decisions of all kinds are deliberated in a *Palaver*, after the ancestral gods have been consulted; in which work is shared out among the sexes and among technico-professional groups.[4]

It would be comparatively easy to dismiss all this as idealism, as seeing Africa through rose-coloured spectacles. It is easy for such ideas to be ridiculed just as it is no doubt easy for their importance to be exaggerated. Yet whether expressed in the idiom of Léopold Senghor or in some other, they reflect a mood which is widely distributed among those who are setting the pace in Africa today. This assertion of his own worth and dignity is the African foundation upon which the whole structure of African life is being built today wherever Africans are free to build it.

Now, very closely related with this discovery both of an African history and an African personality is the need for a group identity. Some words of a shrewd and experienced American investigator, Harold Isaacs of the Massachussetts Institute of Technology, will put the African need in the wider context of our time, and, incidentally, indicate one of the good things which belong to nationalism. After referring to the African's discovery and reassertion of his own history he continues:

Closely bound up with history are the elements of *nation—* nationality, nationalism, national consciousness. I use all three terms because some group identity crises rise distinctively out of each of these variations in a common area of identity. Political upheavals in our decades produced millions of people who came to be known as 'displaced persons', people who suddenly discovered, as Hannah Arendt has pointed out, that nationality had become almost the only link between a person and the rest of humanity, and that to be without it was to be cut off from other men, indeed often cut off from life itself. In addition to stateless

[4] From a speech by Léopold Senghor at Oxford University, October 20th, 1961. This whole range of ideas has been studied at length by Janheinz Jahn in *Muntu, an Outline of Neo-African Culture* (Faber and Faber, 1961).

people in a world of multiplying states, we also now have people, like the Chinese in Malaya or Indonesia, whose problem of nationality has suddenly become a central problem of existence; or like the Jews who in Israel are trying to solve *their* problem by acquiring a nationality distinctively their own. The historically tardy triumphs of nationalism in the last two decades have changed the political face of the world, bringing into being some sixty new nations—some as the products of long struggle, some of no struggle at all. In virtually all of these the first task of the new man of power is to create a new *national identity* that their fragmented peoples will recognize and accept.[5]

There is much in that quotation which is germane to our subject. Amongst much else it points to one explanation of the enormous emotional content of the nationalism of the new nations. For there is a deeper sense in the term 'displaced persons' than is to be found solely in the tragedy of the world's political refugees. When an old pattern of life is almost totally disintegrated by alien forces which by their very power fascinate and yet terrify, there is a vast mass of 'displaced persons', persons whose traditional security, whose sense of being fixtures in a fixed society, has been destroyed. In such case are very large numbers of the people in the newly independent countries, not least in Africa. As Harold Isaacs says, 'to create a new national identity' for such people must be one of the first tasks of the new rulers. There was, I believe, no intentional blasphemy when Dr Nkrumah had the inscription made on the base of his statue in Accra: 'Seek first the political kingdom. . . .' No doubt there are all the makings of a religion of nationalism latent in that inscription. There is much in the adulation offered to Dr Nkrumah which points in this direction. But at least we must take seriously the task which faced him, and which faces other rulers of the new nations in Africa who have to deal with 'their fragmented peoples'.

[5] Harold Isaacs in *The Bulletin of the International House of Japan,* April 1964, pp. 23-24.

In Africa, in particular, we have to remember that society is fragmented into innumerable tribes, each a self-contained entity, naturally suspicious of all other tribes. The European powers, when they began their 'scramble for Africa' drew the boundaries of their colonies without any regard to the peoples who inhabited them. Nigeria, for instance, is a name given to an area which corresponds to no ethnic distinctions whatever. Within its boundaries are three main racial groups and hundreds of tribes. It is true that Britain helped to create a nation by training a civil service in which the principle obtained of the civil servants being moved all over the country. In this way men with a limited tribal background became aware of themselves as part of something greater than the tribe. But that 'greater something' was still the construction of an alien power. On independence the primary task of the government was to create a Nigerian nation, and that task is still to be completed.

Again, if we accept the desirability that the Gold Coast should become the nation of Ghana then it is difficult to see how Dr Nkrumah could do otherwise than fight tribalism as the real enemy of nationhood. A one party state is not, in itself, a denial of democracy. That highly sophisticated form of democracy with which we are familiar, in which the Leader of Her Majesty's loyal Opposition is paid to oppose Her Majesty's Government, is not the only form of democracy. The African tradition, for instance, by which you achieve unity as a result of a long drawn-out palaver is quite as democratic, and may be more democratic, than counting heads when the House divides. In saying that I am not suggesting that African rulers are any more immune from the delights of dictatorship than men of other races, but only insisting that we should not make our western practices into patterns relevant for all times and places.

What is as important as understanding that Africa is going

to work out her own pattern of government, and will do so partly as an assertion of her own self-hood which she is now free to express, is understanding that nationhood in Africa is only a middle-term between the fragmentation of tribalism, on the one hand, and some larger unity than is at present provided by most of the newly independent states. The average population of the newly independent states of Africa is a little over four million persons, a number far smaller than many of the world's great cities. Such units are not economically viable, and for that reason they are unlikely to be politically viable either. If a United States of Africa is still a long way off, yet it may be expected that large regional groupings will emerge before many years have passed. This is the inwardness of the appeal which Pan-Africanism has for many thoughtful Africans. The quarrel between President Nyerere of Tanganyika and President Nkrumah of Ghana at the Cairo All-Africa Conference of Heads of States in July 1964, a quarrel highlighted in the world's press, was a quarrel about the pace towards the goal rather than about the goal itself. President Nkrumah wants a United States of Africa *now*. President Nyerere wants regional groupings as soon as possible as a preparatory stage. If this is an accurate analysis then we must reckon that African nationalism will be an erratic element in the international scene for a long time to come. But this does not mean that it can be ignored. It is already demonstrating that it can be another religion for a race already disposed to be religious.

The Arab Awakening

There is another sense in which nationalism can have religious overtones, and that is when it is a response to fear. This has been latent in much that has been said so far. It becomes quite explicit when we come to study the Muslim world during the last century, with particular reference to its relationship with the western world.

No one can read anything written by the leading personalities in the Arab 'awakening' and not see how hag-ridden they were by fear of the West. No doubt the memory of the Crusades had never faded. No doubt the fact that the Crusades were in part at least a counter-attack in response to Islam's threat to the integrity of Europe was also conveniently forgotten. But in the nineteenth century the situation was different. Everywhere Islam as a religious force was in decay. Sectarianism was rife. The caliphate was exercised by the Sultan of Turkey, a stranger to the heart-lands of Islam, one who could not speak Arabic and therefore could not be the agent of a spiritual revival among those who spoke the language of the Holy Qur'an. And even the Arabic language was degenerating into a number of vernaculars which lacked the inspirational power of the classical age. Upon an Islam where there was so much decay it looked as if the West was about to descend in conquest.

In the first half of the century the predominantly Christian parts of the Ottoman Empire in Europe had begun to revolt, and it was obvious that these revolts had the sympathy of the European powers. It is easy for us of the West to think of the Greek War of Independence as just one more episode in the epic story of eternal Hellas. So Byron saw it and went to join the Greeks and died at Missolonghi in 1824. To Muslims Byron's *Childe Harold's Pilgrimage*, with its lament for the bondage of Greece, would be seen simply as an invitation to rebellion, which of course it was. But the nervousness of the Muslim world at the successive inroads of the West on the Ottoman Empire in the first half of the nineteenth century was nothing compared to the anxiety generated by the occupation of Tunis by France in 1881 and of Egypt by England in 1882. Albert Hourani sums up this anxiety in words we must

I

imaginatively try to understand, if we are to understand the subsequent history of Islam, and most of the political events in the Middle East down until today.

> For a Muslim . . . whether he was Turkish or Arab, the seizure of power by Europe meant that his community was in danger. The *umma* (*the Society of Muslims*) was, among other things, a political community expressing itself in all the forms of political life, and a community which has no power may cease to exist. The problem of inner decay still exercised men's minds, but there was grafted on to it a new problem, that of survival: how could the Muslim countries resist the new danger from outside?[6]

There will be no understanding of nationalism as the Muslims experience it, no understanding the Arab 'awakening', no intelligible interpretation of the politics of the Middle East, which overlooks the enormous tenacity with which the Muslim views the Community of Islam, and the ingrained suspicion he has of all who are not of his Community. For the Muslim, the division of the world into 'The House of Islam', on the one hand, and the rest comprised under the title 'the House of War' is an absolute division which goes to the very roots of his faith. He may—if he is a very advanced thinker, and there are such today—insist that all men are Muslims but they don't know it, and it is for the Muslim who knows he is a Muslim to convince the others. This is the propaganda line sometimes adopted by the heretical Muslim sect of the Ahmadiyyah, a line which has some interesting parallels in Christian thought. But this approach is exceptional among Muslim thinkers. Hence a threat to the Community of Muslims really is a threat to their religion.

And because for the Muslim his Community and his faith are two aspects of the same thing, he assumes that this applies in the western world. There is nothing in Islam which corre-

[6] Albert Hourani, *Arabic Thought in the Liberal Age*, pp. 103-104.

sponds to what we are familiar with as 'the autonomy of the secular'. The principle of toleration as it has slowly emerged in the West, by which a man's religious faith does not affect his rights as a citizen, is quite different from the Muslim interpretation of toleration. The Muslim, as history demonstrates, can be very tolerant indeed. The Islamic form of toleration is to treat those who are non-Muslims as being themselves 'communities', which live according to their own laws. This they are free to do, though by right of conquest the Muslim has claimed a first-class citizenship for himself, and relegated others to a second-class citizenship. Within these limits, however, the second-class citizen has very real freedoms.

Holding such views about the identity of community and religion, the great fear of the Muslim when faced with western aggression has been a fear that he would be compelled to become a Christian. This is the recurrent theme wherever in the nineteenth century there is an encounter between the western world and the great ethnic religions. The founding of the Brahma Samaj in India and the subsequent Hindu renaissance was sparked off by the threat of a widespread attempt to convert Hindus to Christianity. One factor at least in triggering off the Indian Mutiny was the sedulously spread rumour that the government was planning to convert Indians by force. In the case of Buddhism it is only necessary to read *The Revolt in the Temple*[7] and *The Betrayal of Buddhism*[8] to see the bitterness with which Buddhists in Ceylon have resented the policy of successive European powers during their centuries of dominion. A simple illustration of this suspicion comes from the Muslim area of Northern Nigeria during the early days of British rule. In a despatch to the then Colonial Secretary, Lord Crewe, Sir Hesketh Bell wrote:

[7] D. C. Vijayavardhana, *op. cit.* (Sinha Publications, 1953), obtainable from The Lake Publishing House, Colombo, Ceylon.
[8] Obtainable from the N.C.C., 490 Havelock Road, Colombo 6, Ceylon.

I am informed by those who know the country well that, in spite of all our efforts to impress upon the chiefs and peoples of the Moslem territories our earnest desire to work with them for their own welfare, all our efforts are viewed with the greatest suspicion. The Fulani especially appear to entertain a deep-rooted distrust of our intentions, and it is, perhaps, only natural that they should hate us for having broken their power, and reduced them to the condition of practical impotence in which they now find themselves. They fear that schools organized by Europeans are an indirect attack on their religion. . . .[9]

That single episode is typical of countless others which have during the past century and a half complicated the relationship of the West with Asia and with those parts of Africa where Islam has been dominant. In all these areas the strong community sense of the ethnic religions instinctively created the suspicion that the impact of the West was essentially a religious threat.

A fascinating subject for study and research is the process by which these ancient religious cultures of the Arab lands, of India, and of the Buddhist countries reacted either to the threat of, or the experience of, western rule and in the process developed or recaptured a genuine sense of nationhood: of how they tried to use their traditional religious outlook to be the cement of the newly awakened national consciousness: and then of how, in a variety of ways, the insidious appeal of the West, its science and ways of thought, eroded the vitality of the old religious faith, and left as a residue the religion of nationalism.

I would not wish to suggest that this development is anywhere complete, nor would I expect that many nationalists in the Middle East, India and Ceylon or Burma would accept my hypothesis, yet. It would seem to be too great a challenge to the integrity of their national effort, and they would hardly

[9] Bell to Crewe, March 30th, 1910, C.O. 446/89, quoted in *Essays in Imperial Government*, p. 75.

be disarmed by an admission that something very like this has happened in the West itself.

At least this can be claimed that in the Middle East something not unlike this has in fact happened. The story of the Arab 'awakening' is at least suggestive. The first stirrings came with the recovery of a genuine pride in the Arabic language, in its classical form, which began in the thirties of the nineteenth century, largely under the impulse of imaginative American missionaries working in Syria in close association with some very remarkable Arab Christians of Syrian background. Pride in the Arabic language soon led to a new interest in the history of Islam and pride in that history. Turkish misrule and the threat of western imperialism combined to create an Arab consciousness which was in part racial, in part linguistic. But the historical circumstances of the time made the Pan-Islamic or Pan-Arabic ideal impracticable. In the sequel the several nationalisms of Egypt, Syria and Wahabi Arabia fought the battle for their own freedom. In the process, otherwise than in Arabia itself, the idea of an Arabic civilization slowly but surely took pride of place over a distinctive emphasis on Islam as a religion. This idea of civilization in turn came to be heavily influenced by western ideas.

One of the more remarkable interpreters of the Middle-Eastern scene is Taha Husayn who was born in Upper Egypt in 1889. Between 1925 and 1950 he was at the very centre of literary and academic life in Egypt, and played his part in politics, to become what he is now, one of the most highly respected of the older generation. For Taha Husayn,

the distinguishing mark of the modern world is that it has brought about a virtual separation of religion and civilization, each in its own sphere. It is therefore quite possible to take the 'bases of civilization' from Europe without taking its religion.

This involves indeed one condition, which is that Egyptians too should be able to make the same separation.[10]

The next stage in this development is, so Albert Hourani suggests[11], a genuine emancipation on the part of the Middle East from any hypnotic fears of the Western world. World War II has revolutionized the world's balance of power and the countries of the Middle East can now play the two great power-blocs off against one another, while they get on with their own social and economic revolutions. What is more, they are no longer hypnotized by the past. Their eyes are towards the future. At this point he gives an illustration which will be both convincing and appealing to those who, like myself, are philatelists. He writes:

If thinkers and statesmen recognized a norm by which their acts could be judged, it was not to be found in the past but in the future. There had been formed an image of the future to direct and inspire actions, and this was symbolized by the change in postage stamps, which no longer showed mosques or sphinxes or kings, but workers and peasants in heroic attitudes, shaking their fists at fate.[12]

It would hardly be an exaggeration to say that even in predominantly Muslim Egypt man's other religion is Nationalism. Perhaps the decisive moment for the Muslim Middle East when this became patent, though the implications of the event took nearly two generations to make themselves felt, was when, in 1915, the Shaik-ul-Islam under German pressure summoned the Muslim world to 'holy war' against Britain, France and Russia. The appeal made no impact, being shattered on the rock of Arab nationalism.

[10] Albert Hourani, *op. cit.*, p. 332, quoting Taha Husayn in *Mustaqbal al-thaqafa*, pp. 54ff.
[11] Albert Hourani, *op. cit.*, in Ch. 13, 'Epilogue: Past and Future', *passim*.
[12] Albert Hourani, *op. cit.*, p. 350.

Christianity and Nationalism

That example drawn from the Middle East illustrates very clearly how a cultural renaissance and a revival of religion can easily result, as they have resulted again and again in our modern world, in what comes very near to being a worship of the nation. For the nation, as Harold Isaacs has said, is the source of that corporate *identity* which men need so desperately. And it must be expected that the new men in power in the new nations, in pursuing their task of creating the new *national identity* will be very suspicious of anything which threatens to break the unity which has been so precariously established, and which any emergency may destroy.

The inner thought of such national leaders has been most brilliantly depicted in a remarkable book by an Egyptian doctor, Muhammed Kamel Hussein, entitled *City of Wrong: A Friday in Jerusalem*. The book is a sympathetic study of the Crucifixion as seen through the eyes of the main participants. It seeks to enter into their minds, and in doing so, reveals the unity of their experience with our own. Of the many portraits in the book none is more brilliantly drawn than that of Caiaphas. One feels one is there watching his mind at work. And it is, of course, the mind of any national leader at a moment of emergency for his nation. So we hear Caiaphas soliloquising about Jesus:

I admire what he proclaims enormously. But I don't want his religion established here among us. In our present emergency what we need most of all is quietness, inner cohesion and unity. I am concerned lest what he says will provoke disruption and division in our ranks.[13]

Brilliantly, if unconsciously, Kamel Hussein has presented us with the position in which Christ in his Church finds himself

[13] Kamel Hussein, *op. cit.* (Geoffrey Bles, 1961), p. 53.

in many countries today, where nationalism has become man's other religion.

But as Christians, who believe that the missionary movement of modern times has been, with all its weaknesses and failures, part of God's providential operation within history, it is important that we should be clearly aware of the fact that Christianity itself has made a very distinctive contribution to modern nationalism, leaving out of account the contribution it can be said to have made earlier towards creating a national consciousness in almost all the European countries.

George Antonius in his classic record of the Arab national movement of the last hundred years[14] has shown the creative rôle played by the Syrian Protestant College, now the American University of Beirut, founded by American missionaries in 1866 as the educational apex to a considerable pyramid of educational institutions founded over the previous thirty years in Syria. Most notable of the achievements of these missionaries was their enthusiasm for the Arabic language, and the inspiration which they gave to countless pupils to recover the use of the language in its pristine purity. The Americans were soon followed by French missionaries. The free play of these two influences made them, in George Antonius's words 'the foster-parents of the Arabic resurrection.'[15]

A subtler contribution may be discerned in the fact that the very appeal of the West, however little it was recognized, did in fact involve a response to basic Christian insights. Some did, in practice recognize this. One of the most vigorous of the Muslim reformers in Egypt, Quasim Amin, a disciple of that modern Muslim prophet, Muhammad Abduh, was in no doubt about this. I quote him again:

It is useless to hope to adopt the sciences of Europe without coming within the radius of its moral principles; the two things

[14] *The Arab Awakening* (Hamish Hamilton, 1938).
[15] George Antonius, *op. cit.*, p. 35.

are indissolubly connected, and we must therefore be prepared
for change in every aspect of our life.[16]

We have already seen something of the influence of Christianity upon Hindu thinking from the early years of the nineteenth century onwards, an influence which is particularly
interesting when it is so continuously revealed by the use of
New Testament language.

From Africa comes the intriguing and quite unambiguous
testimony of Ndabaningi Sithole of Southern Rhodesia. In his
book *African Nationalism* he devotes a large amount of space
to the decisive contribution made by the Christian missionary
movement to the growth of the nationalist movement. First
came the creation of literacy, everywhere pioneered by missionaries, and then the translation of the Bible with its liberat-
ing power. 'The missionary came in time and laid explosives
under colonialism,' he writes. 'The Bible is now doing what
we could not do with our spears.'[17] The development of a
strong Christian consciousness on the worth and dignity of
the individual was fostered by the spread of education. 'The
Church may be regarded as the guardian angel of African
nationalism. Practically all important African political leaders
went through Christian Church Schools.'[18] According to this
author, the missionaries made a considerable contribution to
the unification of Africa, and by encouraging the study of
European and English history they drew attention to a record
of struggles for liberty.

In this last connection a delightful illustration may be
quoted of how history can achieve an African flavour. In
one mission school there was an occasion of tension and a list
of grievances was presented to the Principal. The spokesman

[16] Quasim Amin, *al-Mar'a*, pp. 198 ff, quoted by Albert Hourani, *op. cit.*,
p. 169.
[17] Ndabaningi Sithole, *op. cit.*, p. 54 and Ch. 5.
[18] Ndabaningi Sithole, *op. cit.*, p. 55.

for the school, one of the senior boys, paused at the end of his speech, bowed to the Principal and concluded with the words: 'Sir, we thought it was right and proper that this matter should be brought before you in this fashion, so that government of the students, by the students, and for the students shall not perish from this Mission Station.'[19]

In listing this evidence I am not suggesting that this record will prompt gratitude. Gratitude is hardly a virtue of politics. Nor do I suggest that it will ensure a continuance of opportunity for the Christian Church. It could well operate to the opposite effect. All I am concerned to do is to indicate how all-pervasive has been the influence of the missionary movement. Its impact has been incalculable, and it has started a chain reaction of effects to which there is no ending.

What, however, is extremely important for us to note is that inevitably the missionary movement is caught up in the effort to determine how much weight must be given to ensuring that the Christian Church is seen to be racy of the local soil, and speaking in a local idiom and accepted as locally relevant, without losing its emphasis on the universals of Christian faith and morals. This is the practical point at which the issue is raised as to how far in the Christian Church in Asia and in Africa (not forgetting the rest of the world) nationalism is the Christian's other religion. The missionary movement of our day stands under the challenge of the words with which the chapter started:

No servant can be slave to two masters; for either he will hate the first and love the second, or he will be devoted to the first and think nothing of the second. You cannot serve God and . . .

19 Ndabaningi Sithole, *op. cit.*, p. 59.

7

THE ORIGINS OF THE ECUMENICAL MOVEMENT

THE *Economist* for July 11th, 1964, had an article with the heading 'The Dynamo of Nations' and a sub-title 'Nationalism is a force for good and evil. Can it be transcended?' In the course of the article came this paragraph:

The question 'What are we to think of nationalism?' seems likely to be with us for some time to come. Nationalism is, at bottom, a highly developed sense of community. The term is usually employed to describe the external manifestations of this spirit; in its domestic form, where it encourages men to sacrifice their individual interests for the common good, it is commonly described as patriotism. The thing in itself is ambivalent. Just as its source may be varied—a common religion or language, or simply a feeling that grows up among inhabitants of the same geographical area—so its effects may range from the creation of national cohesion to the perpetration of external aggression.

The article raised the possibility that some of the dangers in nationalism could be neutralized if it proved possible to develop regional groupings. But this is a long hope. The article ended with the words:

For the moment the shock therapy nationalism brings to new nations can hardly be dispensed with. In the future it may be; but if and when each regional state comes into being, it will have to find a unifying spirit that does not make it glower over the ramparts at its neighbours.

This chapter will be concerned to see if, perhaps, the ecumenical movement within the Christian Church of the world offers some prospect of providing this unifying spirit. It would be rashly optimistic to affirm that it does hold out such promise in any significant measure. Yet in the long span of history we can see that there are forces at work operating towards the creation of a commonwealth of mankind. Modern communications, wireless, the spread of a common scientific culture, these are potential instruments for the creation of such a commonwealth, even if we can claim no more for them than that. The ecumenical movement is another such phenomenon. And it may be that, as we trace the changing usage of the word, we will discover at least one constructive movement in our world which should command our support.

The Origins of 'Ecumenical'

The word 'ecumenical' derives from the Greek word *oikoumene*, which means the inhabited world. But it is important to notice that in their use of it the Greeks were being arrant snobs. What they really meant was the world in so far as it was inhabited by Greeks. The 'rest' were barbarians and did not count. The word, therefore, began with a strictly limited meaning.

But the conquests of Alexander the Great and the spread of Greek ideas widened the connotation of the word to include such parts of the world as were prepared to be influenced by Greek ideas. This was a more generous use of the word and as such it was taken over by the Romans. So it was that Caesar Augustus could send out a decree that 'all the world should be enrolled' and the word for world is *oikoumene*. The Roman Emperor became the *kurios tēs oikoumenēs*—the lord of the inhabited earth. It was, however, still a snobbish word. The people who lived outside the world of the Caesars, the ancestors of the Indians and Chinese, Russians, Scandinavians, the Celts of Northern Scotland and Ireland, did not belong to the inhabited earth. Even when the strictly 'unecumenical' Scottish highlanders defeated a Roman army in the Grampian mountains, the Romans did not allow themselves to change their vocabulary.

The next change, at first a small one, occurred when Constantine made Christianity the official religion of the Roman Empire. The Christian Church became the State Church, and the term 'ecumenical' became related to the ecclesiastical establishment. Hence it is that the seven great Church Assemblies which met between 325 A.D. and 787 A.D. are known to historians as the Ecumenical Councils.

Nevertheless, we must recognize that the use of the term was still a narrow one. The Church of the Ecumenical Councils was the Church of the Roman Empire. 'Ecumenical' was a term which was, so to speak, fenced in. It denoted a geographical area, even when it also indicated a religious allegiance.

Curiously enough, it was the first major division in the Christian Church, the one which followed the Seventh Ecumenical Council, which began to hint at a new meaning for the word 'ecumenical'. After that Council, the Eastern half of the Mediterranean world looked to the Patriarch of Constantinople as its leader, and the Western half looked to the Bishop of Rome. Now the Patriarch of Constantinople assumed the title *Ho Oikoumenikos*—the Ecumenical One *par exellence*. It was a claim to spiritual dominion which refused to be reconciled to any geographical limitations. In the Roman Church, likewise, the Pope came to be referred to as 'The Ecumenical One' and this signified a similar refusal to accept any geographical limitations.

This was only a hint, and it arose out of an unhappy chapter of history, but the word was beginning to move in the right direction. It was still snobbish—ecclesiastically snobbish—but it was snobbery of a kind that could be redeemed, whereas the old Greek use of the word was strictly intolerable and could have no future.

Before following our word any further, it is important for our whole subject to realize that it is of the very heart of the New Testament doctrine of the Church that the Church is a Unity. The Church is the Body of Christ. 'Is Christ divided?' asks Paul of the Corinthians in the very context of a tendency towards division within the Church.

In his very sobering study of Christian disunity, *Schism in the Early Church*, Professor Greenslade makes very clear how tenacious the Church was of its unity, even when it was most tragically divided. As he says:

It was held on biblical grounds not simply that the Church ought to be one, but that it is one, and cannot but be one.

And he goes on to make clear that in the judgment of the early centuries:

This unity was predicated of the visible Church, and the visible Church was thought of organically as one structure, one communion. To their minds divisions, breaches of communion, were not embraced and overcome by a spiritual and invisible unity, nor could a number of denominations aggregate into one Church. There was but one visible Church in one communion; bodies separated from that communion were outside the Church.[1]

Dr Greenslade reminds us of the great concern of the Fathers on this issue:

'Nothing angers God so much as the division of the Church,' says Chrysostom. 'Even if we have done ten thousand good deeds, those of us who cut up the fulness of the Church will be punished no less than those who cut his body (i.e. literally, at the Crucifixion). Not even martyrdom can wipe out that crime.' And Augustine again: 'There is no just necessity for dividing the Church, schism surpasses all crimes, it is *sacrilegium immanissimum* (the most horrible sacrilege).[2]

[1] S. L. Greenslade, *op. cit.*, p. 18.   [2] S. L. Greenslade, *op. cit.*, p. 32.

Yet that same Augustine found himself confronted by the actual fact of schism which, in the sheer logic of his thought, compelled him to look afresh at the whole question posed by Baptism and by the ordered ministry. There is only Christian Baptism, so he affirmed, and Christ himself is the Minister of the Sacrament, a conception which applied, of course, to all sacraments. It was through the Donatist schism that Augustine's thought moved towards the realization that a hard and fast division between those 'inside' and 'outside' the Church was too rigid. Here was the faint first beginning of the recognition that the unity of the Church in a sinful world is a more complicated reality than can be expressed in terms of a common obedience to a single authority.[3] Implicit in Augustine's accommodation to the factual situation was the ultimate emergence of the ecumenical movement we know today, though theologians then and now have put up a formidable resistance. As we shall see, the crucial question is still unresolved: 'What is the nature of the unity we seek?' With this goes the subsidiary question, which takes us back to the New Testament: 'Is organic unity only of one possible kind, to be structured according to only one possible pattern?'

Missionary and Ecumenical Growth

From that important reference back to the New Testament and the early Fathers, we can return to the historical development of the word 'ecumenical'.

For many centuries Western Europe was an island isolated from the rest of the world by the ocean, by the vast steppes of Russia, and by the formidable barrier of the Muslim world. There might be Christians outside Europe—as there were indeed in Central Asia, and South India, as well as in the Middle East, and in what is now the Sudan. But the narrow world of the European Middle Ages gave them very little thought.

[3] S. L. Greenslade, *op. cit.*, pp. 174-175.

Eastern Europe was in large measure dominated by Islam. It was the Holy Places, not the holy brethren, which were the objective of the Crusaders. What is more, much of Eastern Europe was also trying desperately to survive under the waves of Tartar and Mongol invasions. It was not an age for much ecumenical imagining, though one Pope exercised his initiative by sending two friars to invite the Khan of the Tartars to become a Christian.

Then suddenly, the windows of Europe were opened. Columbus, Cabot, Diaz and da Gama showed just how wide the world really was. Drake circumnavigated it in 1580. And it is in the sixteenth century that the word 'ecumenical' is first used in English with its meaning 'world-wide'. There was nothing limited or narrow about this use. And if its first use was essentially geographical, at least it referred to the whole inhabited world, including all the barbarians in it.

There is a nice universal note reflecting something of this new understanding of the world in a Letter Missive which Edward VI sent

to the Kings, Princes and other Potentates inhabiting the mighty Empire of Cathay, at such time as Sir Hugh Willoughby, Knight, and Richard Chancelor with their company attempted the voyage thither in the yeere of Christ 1553.

The Letter Missive spoke of the providential ordering whereby 'not all things should be found in one region, to the end that one should have need of another', and that 'by the friendly means and passage of trade, searching and carrying both over the land and the sea, friendship may be established among all men, and everyone seek to gratify all, to their own mutual benefits and peace'.[4]

---

[4] Richard Hakluyt, *The Principle Navigations, Voiages, Traffiques and Discoveries of the English Nation* (eds. G. Bishop, R. Newberie and R. Barker, 1598-1600) vol. i, p. 226.

We will be right in assuming that the Christian mind has ever been haunted by the conviction that the Church is meant to be a unity. From one point of view the Reformation can be seen as being essentially a challenge to what was held by the Reformers to be an inadequate basis for that Unity. Whatever we may think of their theological arguments, this at least can be said, that the enormous widening of the extent of the world opened up by the voyages of explorers did at least point towards the need to rethink the form of Christian unity. Nor were such efforts wanting.[5] Nevertheless it remains significantly true that the main root from which the ecumenical movement, as we know it today, has sprung, is the missionary expansion of the Christian Church. We have already, in these chapters, noted the inescapable ambivalence of that movement. Yet, when every allowance has been made for the unworthy elements in the expansion of Christianity, some claim can be fairly made that its direction has been constructively intended and has, in fact contributed to the growth of a genuine Christian ecumenicity.

It was, after all, missionaries of the Gospel who first carried the good news of Jesus Christ to every part of the world, and who in a geographical sense of the word made Christianity an ecumenical religion, that is, a religion which is world-wide in its range of influence.

The finger of criticism can, of course, be pointed at these first missionaries who went as virtual crusaders with the Spanish and Portugese explorers. Their spiritual commission may have been to 'convert the Moors' but this could hardly be attempted until the 'Moors' had been brought to submission by the soldiers and sailors who accompanied the explorers.

It is also true that the chaplains who went out under the East India Company did, in practice, confine most of their efforts

[5] For a comprehensive study of these, see *A History of the Ecumenical Movement*, ed. Ruth Rouse and S. C. Neill (S.P.C.K., 1954), pp. 27-120.

K

to their fellow-countrymen, though their terms of reference were wider.

But all this was during the early stages of the expansion of Europe. A much more specific missionary enterprise took shape in the seventeenth century, the initiative coming from John Eliot (1604-1690), a pioneer missionary among the Indians of North America, who was also a pioneer of Church Unity. Against the background of New England his ecumenical concern was first directed to forwarding a union of Presbyterians and Congregationalists, the better to carry on missionary work among the heathen and, as he added, in 'professing nations where there is darkness'. What is intriguing is to note that Eliot envisaged a 'Communion of Councils'. 'In a most original way he sketched out a union plan involving four orders of councils: District (monthly) councils, Provincial (quarterly) councils, National (yearly) councils, and to top his structure, an "Oecumenical Council", which was to be in continuous session at Jerusalem'.[6]

Nothing at the time came of this broad vision, indeed, it could hardly have done so. We need to remember that the ecumenical movement, as we know it today, has only been made possible because of modern means of communication. One hundred years after John Eliot, William Carey was to urge the desirability of a world Missionary Conference to be held in 1810. It is interesting that his very practical mind, alive to problems of communication, suggested that the Cape of Good Hope should be the rendezvous. But the time was still not ripe for any so ambitious a design.

Meanwhile, the real initiative was to rest with the enthusiasm of missionaries in making sure that the expansion of the Christian Faith should be indeed world-wide. And here pride of place must be accorded to the Moravians. In the most recent biography of Zinzendorf there is a moving passage describing

[6] *A History of the Ecumenical Movement*, p. 227.

the 'sending forth' of the first foreign missionaries from Herrnhut. In its simplicity it reflects something which has remained at the heart of the missionary movement ever since.

At three o'clock in the morning of 21st August, 1732, Dober and Nitschmann stepped into a carriage outside Zinzendorf's house. The count drove them the fifteen miles to Bautzen. There they knelt by the roadside. Zinzendorf drove back to Herrnhut; the other two brethren set out on foot for Copenhagen, bundles on their backs, thirty shillings in their pockets, and the invincible all-embracing love of Christ in their hearts. Thus the modern world-wide missionary movement was born.[7]

If that last sentence demands qualification from the historians, yet in that picture of the first Moravian missionaries setting off at 3 a.m. on 21st August, 1732, to walk half across Europe before setting sail to the West Indies we have an authentic glimpse into that astonishing phenomenon of devoted self-sacrifice which has been the real secret of the expansion of Christianity.

Side by side with this spiritual ebullience we must recognize another strand in the story of this expansion, a strand which marks the ambiguous character of the missionary movement, already noted in other contexts in earlier chapters. In this case it is the attempt to export an ecclesiastical establishment already familiar in the country from which the missionaries or chaplains first came. In the case of the Roman Catholic Missions it was in fidelity to their conception of the Church that all the new Christian communities should be welded into that unity which looked for direction to the Pope. What was as intriguing in its ecclesiastical imperialism was the attempt to export the Church of England as by law established. That this attempt at export was always haphazard in the extreme,

[7] A. J. Lewis, *Zinzendorf the Ecumenical Pioneer: A Study in the Moravian Contribution to Christian Mission and Unity* (S.C.M. Press, 1962), pp. 79-80.

and seldom pursued with consistency, is due in the main to the fact that the history of the Church of England since the Reformation has been so largely determined by the course of events within England itself. By the time that the Church of England became even in the smallest degree interested in its missionary duties, its position as an Establishment had diverged a very long way from its originally intended monopoly. Since St Bartholemew's day, 1662, the Church of England, however privileged, has been only one of many denominations in England itself, and overseas has been seldom 'established', and only occasionally in a majority position. This fact has curiously enough made it possible for it to play a part in the ecumenical movement of the last fifty years out of all proportion to its size. But that is another matter.

Meanwhile, there was an undoubted attempt to export the Established Church of this country to other parts of the world, and to do so in terms of an Establishment of religion. Virginia and the Carolinas in North America were one such experiment. The complicated and much disputed endowment of the Anglican Church in Canada, as provided for by the Act of 1791, created as it did a quasi-establishment. This was so tenaciously maintained by Bishop Strachan of Toronto as to present a major political problem which was only resolved in 1854.[8]

The East India Company Act of 1813, which provided for an 'Establishment' in India, albeit the term was used in a limited sense, did nevertheless give the Anglican Church in India a privileged position, not least economically, which remained until 1947.[9] There remains also a wide field for re-

[8] See John S. Moir, *Church and State in Canada West: Three Studies in the Relation of Denominationalism and Nationalism, 1841-1867* (University of Toronto Press, 1959).

[9] The Revenues of the Indian Government as late as 1947 contributed £285,597 to the up keep of the 'Establishment', the greater part going to the Church of India, Pakistan, Burma and Ceylon, an autonomous Province of the Anglican Communion.

search into the Jurisdiction of the Bishop of London, which has never been fully studied, but which is relevant to this theme. And the history of modern Africa provides abundant evidence for the fact that the Anglican Church, as it came into existence in areas of British control, derived very considerable advantage from the fact that the 'Mother Church' was the Established Church in England. This is another fascinating subject waiting for fuller study.

But although we must recognize that ecumenical imperialism, of one kind or another, has been an element in the story of the expansion of Christianity, and still remains the principle obstacle to Christian unity, there was much else that pointed forward to greater ecumenicity.

The Evangelical awakening, whether in America, on the Continent of Europe or in Britain, everywhere led to a new concern for evangelism on a world scale. And because the Churches were, for the most part, deeply suspicious of any form of religious enthusiasm, the new zeal for mission was channelled into voluntary societies. A fact often forgotten is that this development had two very important results. It safeguarded the main stream of missionary endeavour from becoming politically controlled, as it would certainly have been, at least in England, if the societies of the Established Church had been sponsored by the authorities of the Church itself. This was at one time a very real danger. The indifference to mission of the Anglican hierarchy at the end of the eighteenth century was strictly providential. Spain, Portugal and Holland have provided solemn evidence of the mischievous results of state-sponsored missions. In the second place, the fact that the missionary enterprise at that time was undertaken by voluntary societies, did in fact make towards missionary co-operation because the majority of these societies had in common the ideas of the Evangelical awakening.

As early as 1825 Anglican, Congregational, Presbyterian

and Brethren missionaries met together in Bombay to found a Missionary Union with the fourfold objective of (1) promoting the discussion of common problems; (2) discovering areas of agreement; (3) finding means of avoiding friction, and (4) arriving at an agreed common standard of requirements for baptism.

Here were Christians of different traditions coming together round a table to discuss how to tackle common problems and to see where co-operation might be possible. Our word 'ecumenical' is beginning to achieve a wholly new dimension.

What began in Bombay in 1825 and spread all over India, was accepted as a method of working in China and Japan, and came to be adopted in Africa. Immediately significant was the response to the third of the 'Bombay' objectives—that of 'finding a means of avoiding friction'. The means found was the principle of comity, whereby the different Missions undertook to respect each others' areas of working.

John Williams, a missionary of the London Missionary Society working in the Pacific, formulated the principle of comity, although the term was not used until much later, when in 1830 he wrote:

Much as I should rejoice in being associated with an Episcopalian, a Baptist, or a Methodist brother, who did not attach primary importance to secondary objects, yet the interests of every Mission, especially in the early years of its progress, seem to me to require another line of conduct. The natives, through comprehending very imperfectly our objects, would at once discern a difference in the modes of worship, and their attention would, of necessity, be divided and distracted. Being also of an inquisitive disposition, they would demand a reason for every little deviation, which would lead to explanations, first from one party, and then from the other, and thus evils would arise.[10]

[10] J. Williams, *A Narrative of Missionary Enterprise in the Southern Islands* (J. Snow, London, 1837), p. 303, quoted by Pierce Beaver in *Ecumenical Beginnings in Protestant World Mission—A History of Comity* (Thomas Nelson, New York) p. 46.

No less a person that Bishop Selwyn of New Zealand stated much later:

We made a rule never to introduce controversy among native peoples. If the ground has been preoccupied by any other religious body, we forbear to enter. And I can speak from observation, ranging over nearly half the Southern Pacific Ocean, that wherever this law of religious unity is adopted, there the gospel has its full and unchecked power.[11]

Those two statements of the principle of comity present the true answer to the superficial and unimaginative criticism, still sometimes heard, of the monochrome character of some Anglican dioceses. They are also an interesting commentary on all those expressions of denominationalism, Anglican and otherwise, which still all too frequently try to insist on a denominational 'presence' everywhere, on the tacit assumption by each denomination that it, and it only, is the true Church and that *extra ecclesiam*, thus interpreted, there is at best doubtful salvation.

That observation, however, is not made in an attempt to maintain that comity is more than an important way-station along the approach to unity. There comes a stage, and it came in some places quite early, when the principle of comity was seen to be no permanent answer. Always there were limits to its application. Roman Catholics, for instance, never recognized it. Nor have the many modern sects, and still less have the 'one man' missions, those curious phenomena from the United States. Great cities were, from the first, recognized as needing some modification of the rule of comity. Obviously the increasing urbanization everywhere means that comity, as geographically determined, cannot be maintained. But the main factor which has operated to bring this particular ecu-

---

[11] G. A. Curteis, *Bishop Selwyn of New Zealand and Lichfield* (Kegan Paul and Trench, London, 1889) p. 152, quoted by Pierce Beaver, *op. cit.*, p. 62.

menical experiment to an end in most places, is the fact of increased mobility on the part of the population, and even extensive migration. Each Church has found itself faced with a real problem of pastoral importance—the following-up of its own migrant Church members.

Yet we must admit that even 'comity', ecumenical in spirit as it was, had within it the seeds of a grave threat to the whole ecumenical movement. It has proved to be a breeding ground of confessionalism, and the excuse for building up denominational empires.

But while, as students of history, we must recognize these ambiguous elements as being part of the whole story of the missionary and ecumenical movement, yet the main direction would seem to be clear. Any doubt as to that must be dissipated by a study of the great World Missionary Conference held at Edinburgh in 1910.

The importance of this conference can be briefly epitomized. It was in the first place a demonstration of a quickened Christian conscience in regard to the urgency of the evangelical task. There was a widespread recognition that comity could not be the last word and that there must be new forms of Christian co-operation to be explored. For some at least of those at the Conference, the Russo-Japanese war and the victory of Japan pointed towards the end of the great era of world-domination by the western nations.[12] This provided an added note of urgency. More important from the ecumenical point of view, Edinburgh 1910 was the first great Missionary Conference at which High Anglicans were present in significant numbers. As important was the fact that the Archbishop of Canterbury was present and himself made a notable contribution to the gathering. In addition there was the much commented-upon decision

---

[12] This was notably the case with W. H. T. Gairdner, to whom was entrusted the responsibility of producing the one-volume popular report of the Conference, *Edinburgh 1910: An Account and Interpretation of the World Missionary Conference* (Oliphant, Anderson and Ferrier, 1910).

of the Conference to appoint a continuation commitee.

The establishment of this continuation committee, and two other facts, shaped the future development of the ecumenical movement. The first fact was the negative one that by agreement there had been no discussion of matters which directly raised issues of Faith and Order. The positive reaction to this deliberate omission was to inspire Charles Brent, the American Episcopalian Bishop of the Philippines, one of the delegates at Edinburgh, to go back to his country to agitate the mind of his Church until, on April 20, 1911, the Episcopal Church adopted a resolution which determined:

that all Christian Communions throughout the world which confess our Lord Jesus Christ as God and Saviour should be asked to unite with the Protestant Episcopal Church in arranging for and conducting a conference based on a clear statement and full consideration of those things in which we differ, as well as those things in which we are one.

The resolution further expressed the hope that from such a conference would come 'a deepened desire for reunion.[13]

For all these reasons the great Missionary Conference of Edinburgh 1910 was to be a direction-finder. Its continuation committee led in due course to inaugurating the International Missionary Council. Bishop Brent's initiative led to the first Conference on Faith and Order which in due course met at Lausanne in 1927. Independently of these developments Bishop Nathan Soderblom of Sweden, deeply disturbed by the tragedy of the first World War, brought into existence a movement designed to agitate the conscience of Christians towards discovering a way through the tangled problems of peace and war, and social and economic justice. This resulted in the Oxford Conference on Church, Community and State, held in 1937. Although this conference at Oxford owed its inception to Bishop Soderblom's initiative, it proved to have a direct

[13] *A History of the Ecumenical Movement*, p. 408.

link with Edinburgh 1910 in the person of its Secretary, Dr J. H. Oldham. Certainly from that moment the three streams of ecumenical concern, represented by the International Missionary Council, the Movement of Faith and Order, and the movement of 'Life and Work' which found its focus at the Oxford Conference, all slowly but surely converged.

Now it was against the background of all that had happened since Edinburgh 1910 and Lausanne 1927, that the great Conference met at Oxford in 1937 and it was there that the word 'ecumenical' came back into currency to denote a movement. One interpretation of the Oxford Conference used these words.

In the generic sense Oxford was Catholic, meaning of course, universal, all-inclusive, interracial, supranational. A beter word, less subject perhaps to misunderstanding, is the one so frequently applied: Oxford was *ecumenical*. That old word from the Greek was reborn and brought back into circulation, along with the fundamental idea for which it stood in the early Christian centuries . . . the idea of the whole household of Faith.[14]

A Movement of Prayer

So far we have tracing the changing content of the word 'ecumenical'. But it would be a serious misunderstanding of the word if it should be dismissed as the slow process by which an idea took shape in a movement and finally crystallized in an institution called 'The World Council of Churches'. We shall miss the dimension of depth in this whole development if we fail to allow for the place of prayer in that development. Prayer for unity is enshrined not only in our Lord's High Priestly Prayer, as recorded in the fourth Gospel, but is implicit in the whole New Testament record. The ancient liturgies of the Church give moving expression to the fact and goal of unity. And the Evangelical awakening of the eighteenth century, to come nearer to our own time, inspired a great

[14] *The Oxford Conference (Official Report)*, Preface to the American Edition, p. vii.

movement of prayer, prayer for mission and prayer for unity.

Jonathan Edwards, the leader of the New England phase of the Evangelical awakening, insisted that the first step towards closer unity must be praying together. This came to be one of the distinguishing characteristics of the Evangelical revival in every country. And this concerted prayer was directed towards the missionary task, and towards unity, as well as towards revival. Haldane Stewart carried Jonathan Edward's ideas a stage forward by organizing a Union for Prayer.

It was a memorable day when he assembled in his rectory in Liverpool, to discuss his plan, such leaders of the Churches as Daniel Wilson, later Bishop of Calcutta; George Burder, Congregationalist, Secretary of the London Missionary Society; Edward Irving . . . at this time still among the Presbyterians; Jabez Bunting, the leading Methodist; and the German, Dr Steinkopt.[15]

The impetus of this Union for Prayer played a significant part in bringing into existence in 1846 the Evangelical Alliance, one of whose most significant activities has been the annual organization of a week of prayer, as a means, among other things, of uniting Christians in prayer.

Meanwhile, in 1840 a Roman Catholic, Fr. Ignatius Spencer, also proposed a Union for prayer for unity. In 1857 the Association for the Foundation of the Unity of Christendom, the first society actually formed to pray for unity, was founded by Anglicans, Roman Catholics and Orthodox. Tragically enough, the Association was condemned in principle by the Pope in 1864, thereby setting the seal on the idea that it was impossible for Roman Catholics and other Christians to pray together, a decision which is being rescinded a century later. Some credit for this thaw must surely go to that great ecumenical figure of the Roman Obedience, the Abbé Paul Couturier. It was his vision and imagination which found a focus for common

[15] *A History of the Ecumenical Movement*, p. 346.

prayer in which all could join in words taken from the Roman Missal, that 'Our Lord would grant to His Church on earth that peace and unity which were in His mind and purpose when, on the eve of His Passion, He prayed that all might be one'.

In this movement of prayer, we find ourselves considering something which, while it is taking place in history, yet cannot be said to be confined to history. Here the eternal and the temporal meet and we find ourselves dealing with the incalculables and the imponderables. Here is the ultimate ground of faith and hope, and no less surely of charity. No last word can ever be pronounced on a movement whose roots are in prayer.

The Question of the Future

With that caution profoundly observed we may ask again the question raised at the beginning of this chapter as to whether perhaps the ecumenical movement of our time offers some prospect of providing that 'unifying spirit' so gravely wanting in the international scene.

In so far as the ecumenical movement has become institutionalized, we must note certain factors about it which may lead us to doubt the likelihood of our being able to give an affirmative answer to our question. There is, for instance, the fact that the World Council of Churches draws its main strength in both personnel and finance from Churches whose power centres are all in the West. The Orthodox contribution may prove not to be all that much of an exception. Only in so far as the World Council of Churches quite deliberately decentralizes its activities, and the regional organizations of Asia and Africa are seen to have actual authority and resources for initiative, will this challenge to contemporary nationalism be effective.

Note must also be taken of the fact that the Roman Catholic Church is claiming the use of the word 'ecumenical' in a sense which is the precise opposite of that for which the World Council of Churches has been contending, and which it has so successfully embodied. Here is the Christian dilemma. All too easily a Church, as well as a Nation can, to quote the *Economist* again, 'glower over the ramparts at its neighbours'. The great spiritual initiative and genuinely ecumenical spirit of Pope John XXIII has still to dismantle the ramparts, an operation which, we should note, has to be undertaken from both sides and at the same time.

In his book *East African Rebels*, Mr Welbourn directs attention to another fact which augurs ill for Christian ecumenical influence in Africa. He writes of the attitude of the Churches, associated with the ecumenical movement, as that attitude is shown towards the Independent African Churches. Whereas within the ecumenical movement

even if its corporate members suspect the validity of one another's ministries, at least their effectiveness is recognized; and especially in the Mission field, they enter into an association, through national councils of Churches, which in many cases is only just short of organic union and frequently extends to a high degree of intercommunion. They are, apparently, unable to regard the independent, African-led, churches with the same charity.[16]

The rapid development of these Independent Churches,[17] and the by no means wholly dissimilar manifestation of the Pentecostal Movement,[18] gives further grounds for doubt as to how far, as at present constituted, the World Council of Churches can speak a word to the nations, which the nations are at all likely to note as deserving attention.

[16] F. Welbourn, *East African Rebels* (S.C.M. Press, 1961), pp. 205-206.
[17] Bengt G. M. Sundkler, *Bantu Prophets in South Africa* (Oxford University Press, 2nd ed., 1961).
[18] Douglas Webster, *Pentecostalism and Speaking with Tongues* (Highway Press, 1965).

These disconcerting realities suggest that whatever may be said of mankind, the ecumenical movement cannot be said to have 'come of age'. It is still, at least in its institutional forms 'trying to find its feet'. Nor need this be surprising, however commonly overlooked, seeing that its institutional form, as represented by the World Council of Churches, only took shape at Amsterdam in 1948.

What is remarkable and full of promise is the considerable record of achievement which has already been achieved. Denominations which had never previously entered into any kind of discussion with one another, are now accustomed to sit round the table together, and not only to discuss their differences, but to plan all kinds of productive action and to carry it into effect. It is, for instance, a remarkable fact that the World Council of Churches has been responsible for finding homes and livelihood for more than 200,000 refugees. And that represents only a fraction of the actual impetus which it has given since the War to the relief of human need.

Again, and in a very different field of activity, it has, through the Churches' Commission on International Affairs, been able to bring an informed Christian opinion to bear on many political issues. Its contribution in this area of human relations, inevitably made 'behind the scenes', is gratefully recognized by the United Nations, and treated seriously in a great many chancelleries.

Perhaps as significant as any other achievement the ecumenical movement is a development which reminds us that the ecumenical movement is not to be confused with, or confined to, the institutions in which it has found expressions. The ecumenical movement is still a movement, and the impulse of this movement is felt in areas remote from Geneva and largely uninfluenced in any direct sense by anything which happens there. For the ecumenical movement is something happening to the Christian mind throughout the world. And in particular, it expresses itself in two ways—in a growing mutual understanding between all who are occupied in the missionary enterprise (beyond, as well as including, all the influences emanating from the Division of World Mission and Evangelism of the World Council); and in the remarkable growth of intra-confessional theological thinking. Christian activity in mission, and Christian thinking in theology are being profoundly influenced by the ecumenical movement. Here is real ground for hope that a 'unifying spirit' can be discovered which, besides being for the unifying of the Church, will also be for the healing of the nations.

8

CHRISTIAN MISSIONS IN THE CONTEMPORARY REVOLUTION

THIS book has been concerned to relate the modern missionary movement with the whole complex of affairs that go to make up the story of our human society. If for the Christian it should be true that *Nil humani a me alienum puto*, then we must accept the implication that the Christian, and perforce his missionary activity, will be inextricably involved in all that concerns human life. This is what incarnation means. Because the missionary movement is a movement of fallible and sinful human beings, even when inspired by the Holy Spirit, there will be much which calls for both humility and penitence. I would, however, protest that the past is in greater need of understanding than of censorious judgment. If by virtue of the fact that we stand on the shoulders of our fathers we are in some respects wiser than they, in respect of hindsight, that does not mean we are any better. We may indeed be under the greater condemnation.

In this last chapter, we turn from considering how yesterday and the day before yesterday have led up to today, and we concern ourselves with peering from today into tomorrow. But tomorrow and the day after tomorrow and all our tomorrows do not any longer 'creep' at Macbeth's 'petty pace'. There is something of the quality of an avalanche about the pace of events in the midst of which we live. The test of our generation is whether or not we can share the faith of the Psalmist that 'the Lord is king, be the people never so unpatient; he sitteth between the cherubims, be the earth never so unquiet'.[1]

Before turning to the subject of this final chapter I would remind the reader of what I said in the Introduction. Quite deliberately I have presented a picture of the last two hundred years very largely against the background of Britain's imperial development and Britain's religious history. The whole canvas is far too vast to take into consideration the missionary enterprise as it has expressed the devotion and enthusiasm of the Churches of the Continent of Europe and North America. What is more, the materials available for research for this wider picture are more difficult to come by in this country. I do not believe, however, that, in essentials, the evidence from other sources would significantly change the picture I have tried to paint. Earlier I quoted a number of paragraphs from Klaus Knorr's volume *British Colonial Theories, 1570-1850*. An American student, on the other hand, seeking to illustrate a similar theme to mine would no doubt find himself quoting Paul Varg's book *Missionaries, Chinese and Diplomats: The American Protestant Missionary Movement in China, 1890-1952*. He would also have to go to the Harvard University Library and delve into the correspondence of the American Board of Commissioners for Foreign Missions, which is preserved there as affording one main source for American foreign policy in the Middle East in the first half of the nineteenth century!

A further limitation in my treatment has been the fact that only incidentally have I referred to the widespread missionary work of the Roman Catholic Church. In part this is due to the fact that during the first part of our period of study Roman Catholic Missions were passing through a period of eclipse, due in large measure to the suppression of the Jesuit Order. But a parallel movement of the Holy Spirit to the one I have described was also taking place in the Roman Church and

---

[1] Psalm 99.1. PBV.

helps to explain the tremendous surge forward of Roman Catholic Missions from the eighteen-thirties onwards. What, however, is important for our subject today is that the Roman Catholic Missions are confronted with precisely the same tests which other Missions are undergoing and, as a perusal of the very valuable productions of the annual *Semaine de Missiologie* at Louvain makes clear, they are no more satisfied that they know the answers than we are.[2]

The missionary movement is considered in this book in terms of mission outside Britain. I do not for one moment underestimate the importance of mission within Britain, but any serious treatment of that subject would distract attention from our present purpose. Bishop Stephen Neill in his recent book *A History of Christian Missions* helps to make a legitimate distinction when he says:

> Churches in the West have recognized that the task of the Church everywhere is essentially the same. . . . But the task is not precisely the same in all parts of the world and in all Christian situations. The first task in the West is the re-Christianization of those immense areas of life which seem to have fallen out of contact with the Gospel. Whether this task is harder or easier than the task of witnessing to the Gospel in a mainly Muslim country it would be idle to dispute; what is important is that it is not the same task. To bring men and women to Christ in the midst of a civilization which has certain roots in the Gospel, in a great city in which there is a church round every corner, is not the same task as the proclamation of the Gospel in an area where it has never been heard before, in a speech in which it has never been proclaimed before, in a society the organization of which has never been touched by Christian influences.[3]

In this book I treat of Missions in the second sense to which Bishop Neill refers. Let there be no doubt at all that the

---

[2] See *Masses Urbaines et Missions*, rapports et compte rendu de la xxie semaine de Missiologie. Louvain, 1956 (Desclée de Brouwer, 1957).
[3] S. C. Neill, *op. cit.*, p. 572.

peculiar strain and stresses, as well as the peculiar satisfactions, of service as a 'foreign' missionary are substantially and significantly different from those of one called to be a missionary in his own country.

The Contemporary Revolution in Asia and Africa

With our definition of 'Christian Missions' clear, we can try to understand the nature of 'the Contemporary Revolution'. At the very outset I would advance the proposition that the *essential* nature of the revolution of our time, as we see it in the continents of Asia and Africa, is neither political, economic, nor social, though obviously it will find expression under those forms. Essentially it is a revolution in the spirit of man—Asian man and African man. I believe that we shall profoundly miss the inner significance of what is happening in our world if we focus attention either on material development or on such a dramatic phenomenon as the revolt against imperialism, viewed as this commonly is in political terms. The enormous emotional force behind the drive for economic advancement, as well as the virulence with which imperialism is everywhere denounced, derives from something that has happened in the spirit of Asian and African man.

This something can perhaps be best summed up in the words of another Psalmist. Whether he was speaking on behalf of a subject people, or only of some depressed part of his own national community we cannot tell. But what he said expresses exactly the prevailing mood which lies behind the Asian and African revolt against the West.

Have mercy upon us, O Lord, have mercy upon us, for we have had more than enough of contempt.
Too long our soul has been sated with the scorn of those who are at ease, the contempt of the proud.[4]

[4] Psalm 123.3-4. RSV.

The main difference between Asians and Africans today and the Psalmist is that they do not invoke the mercy of God but have taken things into their own hands.

I do not know how to document my conviction on this point, the evidence for which is overwhelming. Shri Panikkar's book *Asia and Western Dominance*, to which I referred earlier, has some striking illustrations. He quotes, for instance, one Foreign Secretary of the former British Government of India as talking of 'the cherished conviction of every Englishman in India . . . that he belongs to a race whom God has destined to govern and subdue.'[5] To that may be added the even more egregious remark of Lord Kitchener, also quoted by Panikkar:

> It is this consciousness of the inherent superiority of the European which has won for us India. However well educated and clever a native may be, and however brave he may have proved himself, I believe that no rank we can bestow on him would cause him to be considered an equal of the British Officer.[6]

Ritchie Calder describes someone whom he encountered during his study of some of the technical assistance projects undertaken by the United Nations Organization:

> X was a western expert, probably the best in his subject in the world but still not as good as he thought himself to be. Nor were the Thais whom he was supposed to be advising as stupid or as ignorant as he insisted they were; indeed, they could have taught him many things he had not bothered to find out. He regarded himself as a sort of Minister Plenipotentiary; he condescended; he dogmatized; he never went out and roughed it with them because, of course, he knew all the answers; he directed operations from his desk; he was a consultant and they must come and consult him.

In short he was everything a technical expert ought not to be

[5] K. M. Panikkar, *op. cit.*, p. 149.   [6] K. M. Panikkar, *op. cit.*, p. 150.

. . . He was a pundit. He was a snob. He was a failure. He was worse than a failure; he was a liability.[7]

Biographies, novels and travellers' tales written over the last seventy years dealing with the white man in Asia or Africa provide similar evidence. Part of the tragedy is that although there were so many white men and women who had a totally different attitude, yet they were a minority. They have not been forgotten in either Asia or Africa, but they could not prevent the revolt against 'the scorn of those who are at ease, the contempt of the proud'.

But the revolution of our time must be understood to have other, and subtler, elements. The drive for economic advancement is inspired by a laudable desire to deal with mass poverty, but it is also an attempt to secure national standing in the world. Consider then the sense of exasperation felt by those who are in revolt against the contempt of the white world, when they find themselves compelled to depend upon that white world for the economic wherewithal to meet even the most modest of their economic ambitions.

Here is a new source of humiliation. It will express itself at one and the same moment by a request for aid and by the deportation of foreigners belonging to the very country from which aid is being requested. That may seem incredibly stupid but it is psychologically understandable, and by Christians, at least, it must be understood. This also explains how, in the jungle of our time, neutralism in international politics is the only possible policy for an economically under-developed country which wants to possess any measure of self-respect and a sense of independence.

Can we be surprised if one incalculable sequel to this complicated psychological condition is a profound suspicion of

[7] Ritchie Calder, *Men against the Jungle* (Allen and Unwin, 1954), pp. 200-201.

neo-colonialism, a chronic anxiety lest the old imperialism may try to return through economic control?

If then we find the cries of nationalism strangely shrill and strident, here, after all, is the explanation. Nor should we be found lacking in sympathy. After all, the nationalism of Asia and Africa is the deposit left by the receding tide of western imperialism. They learnt nationalism from us.

I have dwelt at some length on these psychological aspects of the revolt against the West, because it is very important indeed for our subject that we realize that something of the same spirit of revolt and suspicion and distrust of the West, and the Church of the West, is to be found among many Christians in Asia and Africa. In the religious sphere the revolt is not indeed against contempt. But it is a revolt against paternalism. In this respect the western missionary partook of the arrogance of the western mind. There was for long, and it still survives more often than we care to admit, a tacit assumption that the Church in Asia and Africa would need the supervision and guidance of the westerner for a very long time. Like Uzzah of old the western missionary tended, with the very best of intentions, to keep his hand on the ark of God to prevent an accident. If only relatively rarely he has suffered the fate of Uzzah that has been due to the mercy of God, and to the patience of the Christians in Asia and Africa!

We must, moreover, take seriously the fact that what we rather easily describe as the 'younger churches' are young only in the duration of their local institutional life. They share with us, neither less nor more, in the whole length of Christian experience from the first day till now. Nor does the Holy Spirit need our mediation by virtue of our greater endowment with his gifts. What seriously complicates the relationship of the western Christian with his brothers of Asia and Africa is that he comes from an affluent society, and they are part of a society, and often a very poor part of it,

which is economically under-developed. A relationship which
is too closely determined by the distribution of material aid,
so that *one* always gives and *the other* always receives, is an
unhealthy relationship. No grandiloquent phrases about
'mutual interdependence in the Body of Christ,' however sin-
cerely intended, and however devotedly matched by responsibility in giving, really mitigates the problem. There is nothing
mutual about an exchange of money and martyrdom!

In saying this I would make clear at the same time that this
whole question is receiving the closest attention of those in
positions of leadership in the Christian Mission whether in the
West, in Asia or in Africa. All are determined to discover how
genuine partnership in real mutuality can be achieved. What
is necessary for our understanding of the missionary movement in the contemporary revolution is an awareness that
there is a real problem and that, for it, there is no easy solution.

Meanwhile the resurgence of the ancient religions of Asia
and Africa, which we have already considered, is in one respect an expression of this revolt against the West. We have
seen this resurgence as having been stimulated by Christian
Missions. But we also need to take to heart the reminder of
Dr Kraemer that:

The peoples of Africa and Asia have their 'Western question'.
We forget this too easily, we who look at this Oriental world as
an 'Eastern question'. Till the end of the Second World War,
'Westernization', for those people which constitute the adherents
of the non-Christian religions, meant a sort of nature event, a fate
which overtook them. They reacted to it, partly willingly, mostly
reluctantly. For them this political and economic dominance was
also an invasion by the West of their cultural and spiritual realm.
To the economic and political 'invasion' they had to submit but
in the cultural and spiritual sphere they could resist, but were
deeply wounded by the pretension of racial and cultural superiority made by the white domination.[8]

[8] Hendrik Kraemer, *Religion and the Christian Faith*, pp. 25-26.

Dr Kraemer goes on to point out that the achievement of independence by these nations has had a twofold result. On the one hand it has enabled them to treat 'westernization' as merely a technical tool which they can use to their own ends. They are eager to see what science and western skills can do to change both nature and man. This is a big change and one which greatly ministers to their self-respect. But, on the other, hand, adds Dr Kraemer:

This change manifests itself in resurgence of their own religious and cultural self-consciousness and in an insuperable resentment against the West, revealing how the insult to their spiritual and cultural pride went to the very quick in the days of overbearing Western dominance.[9]

It is not altogether surprising that one manifestation of this recovery of cultural and religious self-respect which has followed upon political independence is a new missionary spirit, sometimes of a very aggressive kind. The Arya Samaj in India, and the Ahmadiyyah movement in Africa, are militantly opposed to Christianity, as, of course, is Soka Gakkai in Japan. In as much as these anti-Christian movements are an expression of this religious revolt against the West, they present the Christian Church in Asia and Africa with new problems, problems which, in the main, can only be tackled with their own spiritual resources and out of their own prophetic understanding of the meaning of the Christian Faith.

The nature of the Contemporary Revolution in Asia and Africa is then, in its very essence, a revolt in the spirit of Asian and African man. But that revolt itself has a context in our world, two aspects of which must be noted, for they are having incalculable consequences for Asia and Africa, their peoples and their religions, as they are having for the peoples of the West.

[9] Hendrik Kraemer, *op. cit.,* p. 26.

There is in the *first* place the rapid spread of what can best be described as a secularist-materialism which finds no necessity for God. To a degree which would seem to have no previous parallel those who are the priests of the new humanity and who set the pattern of human thinking believe in the self-sufficiency of man. This is a new kind of man. Among the Dead Sea scrolls there has been discovered a text which has this literal rendering of Habakkuk 1.11 : 'This man makes his strength his God'. Man has always tended towards such self-sufficiency. Adam fell for the idea in the Garden of Eden. But to a degree which has no obvious precedent this is the widespread faith of multitudes, and more particularly of those who shape the climate of contemporary opinion. What this challenge will mean for the ancient religions of Asia and Africa we do not know. Most of us have our hands full with what is its immediate impact upon Christianity. For them and for us this is part of the context of our world. Immediately, the leading thinkers of Hinduism, Buddhism and Islam are insisting that their philosophies give a better answer than does Christianity. This is another element in their opposition to Christianity.

In the *second* place, immensely relevant to the Christian missionary task is the paganization of so much of our western life, or perhaps, out of respect for paganism which after all has a specific religious content, we should say the widespread loss of a religious sense on the part of western man. Whilst writing this chapter I had before me a letter from a missionary in the Middle East:

One particular concern on my mind is the apparent discrepency which exists between the Gospel which we carry and the culture from which so many of the Gospel-bearers come, and which one believes is one of the chief factors preventing Africans and Asians from hearing what the Christian Church is trying to say. This is chiefly seen in the unrestrained sexual paganism which appears in Western films, magazines, etc., and which is in sad contrast with the restraint practised in Islam, but at a far deeper level it is discernible in the comparative absence of religious sanctions noticeable in the behaviour of Europeans in general.

He adds:

The resolving of this discrepancy and the recovery by the Churches of the West of a proper and unequivocal relationship to their own societies is as important an issue and as critical a one as any other that I can think of—as important as the recruitment of missionaries or of funds.

The Prospects for the Foreign Missionary

In a sense which has no historical precedent, this has become one world. Modern means of travel and the use of wireless for communication combine to make us all neighbours, uncomfortably close neighbours. Countries may still seek to escape into isolation but that way of escape is an illusion. Meanwhile our new neighbours are sometimes extremely uncongenial because their customs differ from ours and their manners derive from strange premises with which we are unfamiliar. We all, our new neighbours and ourselves, are going to be called to undertake a mission of practical friendliness which will be extremely demanding. Here is a new aspect of mission, in which Christians will find themselves involved and in which they will discover many helpers in men and women of goodwill who are not Christians but who genuinely share in this aspect of mission. The significant pioneering of this field by the various agencies operating for the relief of refugees, and such far-ranging service as that offered by Christian Aid, Oxfam, and 'Amnesty' are opening up new creative possibilities for service. These possibilities may in some degree mitigate the negative and destructive aspects of the revolution of our time and prepare for the work of construction which, if history is to continue, will certainly follow.

There are those who may well think that this philanthropic enterprise which I have just sketched is the modern form of mission *par excellence* and that what has hitherto been viewed as the missionary programme of the Church is now out-of-date. Such a conclusion, tempting as it may be to some, ignores the very heart of the Christian Gospel, which is that God, who has revealed himself in Jesus Christ, seeks to bring the whole human family into fellowship with himself. Breaking down the barriers of separation and meeting material needs are corollaries of the Gospel. The Gospel itself is a revelation which invites to faith and demands decision, and that faith and that decision need to be sustained by worship, obedience and fellowship. The Christian mission is concerned with this Gospel and with demonstrating that it is a living reality expressed in a way of life.

For such a mission men and women will be needed. What must surely stand to reason is that they must be men and women of a certain temper of mind and quality of spirit which will be able to cope with the intricate problem of living in an alien environment and sharing with fellow-Christians in that environment in their task of witness to the Gospel, and in some cases no doubt being prepared to go to places where there are no fellow-Christians at all. Earlier in this chapter occurred the phrase, 'There is nothing mutual about an exchange of money and martyrdom'. It is a harsh phrase. It needs exposition. The phrase was used in relation to the question of mutuality, of Christians in one part of the world both giving to and receiving from Christians in another part. By way of illustration we may think of the Kikuyu Christian martyrs at the time of Mau Mau. All who heard anything of their story of devotion unto death must have been inspired and strengthened in their own discipleship. We in this country *received* much from that martyr church, more than we can easily repay. Can anyone seriously imagine that mutuality in such a case can be met by our sending money and nothing but money to that Church? The word 'martyr' derives from the Greek word meaning 'witness'. And a witness is a person who may have to give his witness up to the point of physical suffering and death. But a man is no less a witness, a martyr, who in St Paul's words 'dies daily'. Mutuality means a sharing in 'witness' and that involves 'witnesses'. Essentially the 'foreign missionary' is a fellow-witness with the members of the local Christian community, as well as a symbol of the world-wide character of the witnessing community.

To be this kind of witness in some other country than his own will make special demands not only on the body but on the mind and the spirit. Before any man or woman can undertake it he must have learnt something of how to rub shoulders with those who have learnt their lessons by a different discipline from his own; he must have begun to learn something of the nature of the revolution in the country to which he is to go; he must have begun to absorb the fundamental truth of just how ignorant he is. Manifestly such a man and such a woman must receive some specialist training before he or she goes overseas. To rebel against that is a primary disqualification for being a witness.

What, then, are the prospects for the foreign missionary? Let it be noted at once that the word 'foreign' does not necessarily denote 'white'. Already there are many Asians and Africans who are acting as missionaries in precisely the same way as missionaries from Europe and America.

I distinguish three 'prospects' for the foreign missionary. *First* there is the prospect of working along lines already widely familiar from past practice. The teacher, the doctor, the nurse, the agriculturalist, the pastoral evangelist, the teacher of theology, to mention the main traditional activities of the missionary—all of these are still needed in one part of the world or another. Those with such qualifications can be sure of being used somewhere, though the particular strains and stresses of their service will be directly influenced, of course, by the Contemporary Revolution.

A *second* prospect, one which, I believe, is going to offer increasing scope for men and women of enterprise and initiative can be described under the heading 'sanctified opportunism'. The scriptural precedent for this is, of course, Abraham 'the nomad of faith' as Buber described him. Such will find new scope in Christian broadcasting overseas, in literature projects, in drama, in industrial missions, and in work camps. For some it may well be that they will go overseas in business contracts or under auspices in no way associated with the Church, but will go with a missionary vocation, and under missionary discipline as regards the rule of life. The 'Little Brothers of Jesus'[10] of the Roman Catholic Church are one illustration of the way in which such a vocation can be served. And there are others, some already being explored, and many other expressions of the same idea which only await the pioneers.

A *third* prospect which may be expected to develop with considerable momentum is offered by international teams, ideally on an ecumenical basis. On a small scale such have existed for some time in Union institutions. What has not yet been devised is a satisfactory system of training for what is in its very nature an extremely difficult and testing form of service. Such teams could be a notable witness to the ability of the Christian Faith to transcend differences of racial background, intellectual discipline, and social habit. If the experiments so far made have fallen short of success it is in the main due to a lack of adequate training for a type of work more demanding than most.

---

[10] For a description of the ideas expressed by 'The Little Brothers of Jesus' see R. Voillaume, *Seeds of the Desert: The Legacy of Charles de Foucauld* (Burns and Oates, 1955).

The New Climate of Mission

Bearing in mind both the fact of the Contemporary Revolution in all its threatening complexity, and the practical considerations just discussed, we are in a position to consider what I would want to call the new 'climate' of mission. By that I mean the new attitude which is increasingly informing the minds of those who are committed to a continued engagement in mission, as we have here defined it.

The Contemporary Revolution in Asia and Africa is most certainly a revolution of resentment, as we have seen. But it is more than this. It is also a revolution of expectancy. We shall misjudge the meaning of events if we fail to see in them the surging of a great hope A few years ago a book was published consisting of speeches by the Philippine Ambassador to the Court of St James, His Excellency Leon Ma Guerrero. In one of these speeches the Ambassador described this revolution of expectancy, and said:

The word I would like you to remember is 'optimism'. Because ancient Asia is reborn, because she is young again, she is full of hope. She is everything that the young are: enthusiastic, quarrelsome, idealistic, impulsive, intolerant, generous in sacrifice, sanguine in expectations, and often divided in heart and confused in purpose by the discovery of reality. Perhaps you will forgive me the indiscretion of saying that, by contrast, it is Europe that seems ancient. To the traveller from Asia, Europe seems old and weary, tired of so much history, tired of making it and enduring it, tired of having so many things happen to her. Europe just wants to be left alone. But young Asia has a lot of history before her; she wants to get so many things done that the past left undone. In terms of history, it is the Asians who are the young Elizabethans, sure of honour and glory, reckless of the odds, enchanted by self-discovery, feverishly impatient of success.[11]

[11] Leon Ma Guerrero, *Alternatives for Asians: The Philippine Experiment* (Philippine Embassy, London, 1957).

What that quotation says of Asia is equally true of Africa.
To match that hopefulness, the Christian mission must
bring its own intrinsic attitude of hope. This Christian hope is
compounded of certainty, clear-sightedness, commitment and
confidence. *Certainty* is based on the God revealed to us by
Jesus Christ. *Clear-sightedness* is well described by that coura-
geous Czeckoslovak Christian, Dr Hromadka:

Hope for man involves a deep knowledge of man's situation, a
self-identification with his weaknesses, dangers, sickness, with
his pilgrimage on a difficult road, and with his striving for human
dignity, freedom, and brotherhood. Hope for man means struggle
for him.[12]

Commitment means obedience without the enfeeblement of
perpetual qualifications. For the real meaning of Christian
confidence I would give you some words of Professor Moule in
his book *The Meaning of Hope*:

Hope is not a calculated security; on the contrary, the first
requisite if we are to possess hope is that we should be dispossessed
of security, and instead should daringly and at absolute risk cast
ourselves trustfully into the deep which is God's character. To
hug the shore is to cherish a disappointing hope; really to let myself go and to swim is to have discovered the buoyancy of hope.[13]

It is this new understanding of hope which is going to
enable the Christian missionary enterprise to enter redemp-
tively into the hopefulness of Asia and Africa, and indeed into
the whole Contemporary Revolution.

With such a hope the missionary becomes a man who is able
to be adaptable to the people he encounters. Mission itself becomes essentially flexible in its readiness to use every means

[12] J. L. Hromadka, 'Hope for Man', an article published in *Student World*
No. 1 1963. Obtainable from World Student Christian Federation, 13 rue
Calvin, Geneva, Switzerland.
[13] C. F. D. Moule. *op. cit.* (Highway Press, 1953) p. 23.

that is consistent with its end. In this regard the missionary finds himself happily in sympathy with all those efforts towards friendliness we have already considered. Wherever men are themselves forthcoming he will meet them more than half way. Where they are suspicious, as they will often be, he will seek to serve them and so disarm their suspicion. Where they are self-confident and even naïve in that 'optimism' which the Ambassador of the Philippines described, he will be understanding. And when he encounters the man whose every action symbolizes his new independence he will respect and not resent him. Those are the basic attitudes of mind which are indispensible for the Christian mission in the Contemporary Revolution. There is nothing distinctively new about them but the circumstances in which these attitudes must find expression are almost completely new.

In these new circumstances we have a new science of understanding, sometimes glimpsed in the past, but only in our generation made widely available. I refer to the composite achievements of anthropology, sociology and psychology, each illuminating and illuminated by the comparative study of man's religious consciousness.

Dr Mircea Eliade, in whose books so much of this new knowledge is presented, reminds us that the revolution of our time has certain practical consequences:

Western man is no longer the master of the world; he is no longer managing 'natives' but talking with other men. It is as well that he should learn how to open the conversation.[14]

To that we may add, what Dr Eliade would certainly approve, that we should also learn how to listen to a conversation opened by some other man, particularly a man who lives by different religious insights from our own.

[14] Mircea Eliade, *Myths, Dreams and Mysteries* (Harvill Press, 1960), p. 38. See also *Images and Symbols* (Harvill Press, 1961), *The Myth of the Eternal Return* (Bollingen Foundation, New York 1954).

Dr Eliade's books are a plea to understand what the other man 'sees' and not to presume, just because the other man and I are looking at the same thing, that we are both seeing the same thing. And Dr Eliade would insist that in trying to see what the other sees I come to understand myself better. The effort to do this, he says, 'is repaid by a considerable enrich-ment of consiousness.'[15] That is a commonplace of effective communication. So easily in our presumption we forget that communication is a two-way process; we forget that it involves meeting. Where there is real meeting those who meet are changed. And the Christian will expect this because he knows that in every genuine conversation the transforming power of the Creator Spirit is at work.

In a letter to a cousin, written while returning to China for further exploration, Père Teilhard de Chardin was comment-ing on the complexity of the different religions, and how hard it was to 'meet' with those who professed them. He used this graphic phrase: 'You feel that you come up everywhere against water-tight bulkheads between minds, and you have to dive down to the absolute depths if you really want to make contact with souls.'[16]

That metaphor of 'diving deep underneath' has an obvious psychological meaning. It refers to that level of consciousness where all men are at one, where we know ourselves victims of a common bondage, of a common situation in our world, of our need for a deliverer, of the way of escape, if only we can discover the sacred place, the tree which reaches to heaven, the Cross. Mircea Eliade is an invaluable guide here as he inter-prets for us the welter of myths and symbols, those archetypes of which Jung speaks, which are the common denominator of men's unconscious minds. The missionary evangelist who is genuinely and sensitively aware of the problems of 'conversa-

[15] Mircea Eliade, *op. cit.*, p. 9.
[16] Teilhard de Chardin, *Letters from a Traveller* (Collins, 1962), p. 124.

M

tion' will find in Dr Eliade's books a gold-mine of illumination
and inspiration for 'deep-diving'.

Christians in Dialogue

The term 'dialogue' is currently fashionable and frequently
misapplied because misunderstood. Dialogue, properly con-
ducted, is not a way of soft-pedalling truth, an easy pursuit of
superficial agreement, a compromise on fundamentals. It aims
at none of these on the part of the Christian, nor expects them
of the Hindu, the Muslim, or the Buddhist or whatever Faith
the other man may hold. Essentially 'dialogue' is an expression
of that inner humility which acknowledges that Truth is
always more than one has yet discovered, and which is prepared to learn more about Truth from the discovery of what
another has found. And this humility is based on the deep
conviction that because Jesus Christ is the Truth no real truth,
wherever discovered or by whomsoever communicated, can
ever be inconsistent with 'the truth as it is in Jesus'.

The way in to 'dialogue' may take various forms. In that
very interesting journal of Christian exploration, the quarterly
bulletin of the Christian Institute for the Study of Religion
and Society in Bangalore, South India, a recent Editorial
spoke of a 'co-operative dialogue in a community of mutual
understanding, personal confidence and common action in
society.' Such a 'dialogue' might arise out of thinking and
acting together about some outstanding social problems in
society. This might well be a prelude to theological dialogue,
be indeed one form of that adventure in 'friendliness' which in
so many places must be the 'way in' for the Christian in his
missionary concern.

More commonly in recent years the notion of 'dialogue' has
been made familiar to many by the writings of Dr Kenneth
Cragg. Quite deliberately he approaches the religious Muslim
by asking what is the truth in those convictions by which the

Muslim lives. The theology behind this approach is based on the belief in the *Logos*, understood as the divine quest for man, which never despairs, and is forever an urgent pressure on the human mind. There is, that is to say, an activity of revelation in which God is always at work as part of that overflowing of divine love which found supreme and unique expression in Jesus Christ. Such a theology is properly speaking a theology of encounter and a theology of hope.

Perhaps Dr Cragg's most remarkable achievement, brilliantly exemplified in his book *The Call of the Minaret*, is the way in which from inside the best of Islam, which is genuinely appreciated as very good, the road is seen to lead into mystery. A similar approach will find the same result in regard to other religions. What the Christian makes as his act of faith is that the mystery is not insoluble. But it is with no pride of possession but only as a fellow-sinner that the Christian invites the man of another Faith to ask whether perhaps after all the revelation of the mystery is not Jesus Christ.

No one will pretend that such an approach will provide an easy programme. What can be maintained is that the principle of such an approach can be applied at every level. To accept the principle is to be living in a new 'climate' in which faith and hope and charity can breathe and make their own impact.

In his book *The Interpretation of the New Testament* Bishop Stephen Neill has a passage, which is the more moving when we remember that he has himself been a missionary in India. He writes:

The missionary is completely immersed in history—not of course in . . . the mere arid succession of the things that come and go. He is engaged the whole time in making history, divine history. Things are happening today which have never happened before. In the mysterious providence of God, peoples which have never heard the Word of God, and were therefore without hope and without God in the world, are today hearing and believing.

In this village and that, the first baptisms have taken place; for the first time since the foundation of the world the table of the Lord has been spread, and the faithful have gathered, as the early Christians did, in the assurance that *Kyrios Christos* is in their midst. These things are not epiphenomena of the Gospel, secondary accretions of little importance. They *are* the Gospel. It is only when these things are taken seriously that it is possible to understand what Paul is talking about in his Epistles; or to go further back, to understand what Jesus Christ means when he claims to be the One in whom uniquely God speaks to all men —'but I say unto you. . . .'[17]

I think that that passage may be said to sum up a very large part of my argument, provided that full value is given to the opening words, 'The missionary is completely immersed in history'; and not only the missionary, but the whole missionary movement in modern history. Let us also take seriously and humbly the spiritually ambiguous fact that the missionary, and likewise the missionary movement, 'is engaged the whole time in making history'. I hope that I have established some of the grounds for making this claim. That granted, we can go on joyfully to accept the truth that there is, indeed, 'a divinity that shapes our ends, rough-hew them how we will'. In and through the history that is made, God reveals himself as working out his purpose for the salvation of all mankind.

[17] S. C. Neill, *op. cit.* (Oxford University Press, 1964), p. 268.

BIBLIOGRAPHY

1 · *Christianity, Commerce and Imperialism, 1729-1834*

WILLIAM LAW, *A Serious Call to a Devout and Holy Life* (Everyman's Library, J. M. Dent, 1940).

NORMAN SYKES, *Church and State in England in the Eighteenth Century* (Cambridge University Press, 1934).

MAXIMIN PIETTE, *John Wesley and the Evolution of Protestantism* (Sheed and Ward, 1937).

ERIC WILLIAMS, *Capitalism and Slavery* (André Deutsch, 1964).

I. R. SINAI, *Modernisation: The West's Impact on the non-Western World* (Chatto and Windus, 1964).

WILLIAM CAREY, *An Enquiry into the Obligations of Christians to use Means for the Conversion of the Heathens* (Hodder and Stoughton, 1891).

KLAUS KNORR, *British Colonial Theories, 1570-1850* (Frank Cass and Co. Ltd., 1963).

ADAM SMITH, *Wealth of Nations*.

EUGENE STOCK, *History of the Church Missionary Society* (C.M.S., 1899).

M. G. JONES, *Hannah More, 1745-1833* (Cambridge University Press, 1952).

2 · *Missionary Motives, 1789-1859*

WILLIAM CAREY, *An Enquiry into the Obligations of Christians to use Means for the Conversion of the Heathens* (Hodder and Stoughton, 1891).

J. EDWIN ORR, *The Second Evangelical Awakening in Britain* (Marshall, Morgan and Scott, 1949).

The Missionary Register for the year 1813 containing an abstract of the Proceedings of the Principal Missionary and Bible Societies throughout the World.

JOHANNES VAN DEN BERG, *Constrained by Jesus' Love—an inquiry into the motives of the Missionary Awakening in Great Britain in the period between 1698 and 1815* (J. K. Kok, N.V., Kampen, Netherlands, 1956).

CLAUDIUS BUCHANAN, *Memoir of the Expediency of an Ecclesiastical Establishment for British India.* (London, 1812).

AINSLIE EMBREE, *Charles Grant and British Rule in India* (Allen and Unwin, 1962).

CHARLES SIMEON, *Memorial Sketches of the Rev. David Brown* (London, 1816).

HENRY MARTYN, *Journals and Letters* (Edited by S. Wilberforce, London, 1837).

Proceedings of the Society for Missions to Africa and the East instituted by Members of the Established Church (London Vol. I, 1801-1805).

RICHARD LOVETT, *The History of the London Missionary Society* (Oxford University Press, 1899).

3 · Christianity and the Third British Empire, 1857-1947

EARL GREY, *The Colonial Policy of Lord John Russell's Administration* (Richard Bentley, London, 1853) 2 vols.

PAUL KNAPLUND, *Gladstone and Britain's Imperial Policy* (Allen and Unwin, 1927).

PHILIP WOODRUFF, *The Men who ruled India—The Founders* (Jonathan Cape, 1953).

G. M. YOUNG, ed., *Speeches by Lord Macaulay with his Minute on Indian Education, selected with an Introduction* (Oxford University Press, 1935).

GEORGE SMITH, *Alexander Duff* (Hodder and Stoughton, 1879).

ROLAND OLIVER, *Sir Harry Johnston and the Scramble for Africa* (Chatto and Windus, 1957).

H. H. JOHNSTON, *The Backward People and our Relations with Them* (Humphrey Milford, Oxford University Press, 1920).

KENNETH ROBINSON and FREDERICK MADDEN, eds., *Essays in Imperial Government* (Oxford, Basil Blackwell, 1963).

MARGERY PERHAM, *Lugard—The Years of Adventure, 1858-1898* (vol. i) and *Lugard—The Years of Authority, 1898-1945* (vol. ii) (Collins, 1956 (vol. i) and 1960 (vol. ii).

S. C. NEILL, *A History of Christian Missions* (Penguin Books, 1964).

4 . The Disintegrating Impact of Westernization

MAURICE ZINKIN, *Development for Free Asia* (Chatto and Windus, 1956).
I. R. SINAI, *The Challenge of Modernization: The West's Impact on the non-Western World* (Chatto and Windus, 1964)
MARGERY PERHAM, *Lugard Vol I—The Years of Adventure, 1858-1898* (Collins, 1956).
S. GOPAL, *The Permanent Settlement in Bengal and its Results* (Allen and Unwin, 1949).
AIDAN SOUTHALL, ed., *Social Change in Modern Africa* (Oxford University Press, 1961).
MAX GLUCKMAN, ed., *Essays on the Ritual of Social Relations* (Manchester University Press, 1962).
K. M. PANIKKAR, *Asia and Western Dominance* (Allen and Unwin, 1953).
GUY HUNTER, *The New Societies of Tropical Africa* (Oxford University Press, 1962).
S. HERBERT FRANKEL, *The Economic Impact on Under-developed Societies: Essays on International Investment and Social Change* (Oxford Blackwell, 1953).
W. F. WERTHEIM, *Indonesian Society in Transition* (W. Van Hoore, The Hague, and Heffers, Cambridge 1956).
A. R. VIDLER, *The Church in an Age of Revolution* (Pelican Books, 1961).
BARBARA WARD, *India and the West* (Hamish Hamilton, 1961).
EGBERT DE VRIES, *Man in Rapid Social Change* (S.C.M. Press, 1961).
PAUL ABRECHT, *The Churches in Rapid Social Change* (S.C.M. Press, 1961).

5 · The Resurgent Religions of Asia and Africa

STEPHEN NEILL, *Christian Faith and Other Faiths: The Christian Dialogue with Other Religions* (Oxford University Press, 1961).
HENDRIK KRAEMER, *Religion and the Christian Faith* (Lutterworth Press, 1956).

A. C. BOUQUET, *The Christian Faith and Non-Christian Religions* (Nisbet, 1958).

P. D. DEVANANDAN and M. M. THOMAS, eds., *Religion and Society* vol. viii, No. 4, Dec. 1961.

EDWIN HATCH, *The Influence of Greek Ideas and Usages upon the Christian Church* Hibbert Lectures 1888 (William and Norgate, London, 1891).

KENNETH INGHAM, *Reformers in India, 1793-1833* (Cambridge University Press, 1956).

D. S. SARMA, *The Renaissance of Hinduism* (Benares Hindu University, 1944).

WILLIAM STEWART, *India's Religious Ferment* (S.C.M. Press, 1964).

S. RADHAKRISHNAN, *Occasional Speeches and Writings*, 1st series 1956, 2nd series 1957 (Publications Division, Delhi).

S. RADHAKRISHNAN, *East and West: Some Reflections* (Allen and Unwin, 1955).

S. RADHAKRISHNAN, *The Hindu View of Life* (Allen and Unwin, 1926).

D. C. VIJAYAVARDHANA, *The Revolt in the Temple* (Sinha Publications, 1953), obtainable from the Lake Publishing House, Colombo, Ceylon.

MAURICE ZINKIN, *Development for Free Asia* (Chatto and Windus, 1956).

ALBERT HOURANI, *Arabic Thought in the Liberal Age, 1789-1939* (Oxford University Press, 1962).

CONSTANCE E. PADWICK, *Muslim Devotions: a Study of Prayer-Manuals in Common Use* (S.P.C.K., 1961).

MUHAMMAD ASAD, *The Road to Mecca* (Max Reinhardt, London 1954).

KENNETH CRAGG, *The Call of the Minaret* (Oxford University Press, 1959).

KENNETH CRAGG, *Sandals at the Mosque* (S.C.M. Press, 1959)

KENNETH CRAGG, *The Dome and the Rock* (S.P.C.K., 1964).

WILFRED CANTWELL SMITH, *Islam in Modern History* (Princeton University Press, Oxford University Press, 1957).

J. SPENCER TRIMINGHAM, *A History of Islam in West Africa* (Oxford University Press, 1962).

HARRY THOMSEN, *The New Religions of Japan* (Charles E. Tuttle Co. Rutland Vermont & Tokyo, 1963).

RAYMOND HAMMER, *Japan's Religious Ferment* (S.C.M. Press, 1961).

GEORGE APPLETON, *On the Eightfold Path* (S.C.M. Press, 1961).

ARON BARTH, *The Modern Jew faces Eternal Problems* (The Religious Section of the Youth and Hechalutz Department of the Zionist Organization, Jerusalem, 1956).

F. W. FOERSTER, *The Jews* (Hollis and Carter, London, 1961)

HERMAN WOUK, *This is My God* (Jonathan Cape, 1960).

JOHN TAYLOR, *The Primal Vision: Christian Presence amid African Religion* (S.C.M. Press, 1963).

JANHEINZ JAHN, *Muntu: An Outline of Neo-African Culture* (Faber and Faber, 1961).

M. J. FIELD, *Search for Security—an Ethno-psychiatric Study of Rural Ghana* (Faber and Faber, 1960).

F. B. WELBOURN, *East African Rebels* (S.C.M. Press, 1961).

B. G. M. SUNDKLER, *Bantu Prophets in South Africa* (Oxford University Press, 2nd ed. 1961).

MAX GLUCKMAN, *Custom and Conflict in Africa,* (Oxford, Basil Blackwell, 1956).

6 · *Nationalism, Man's Other Religion*

HARRY THOMSEN, *The New Religions of Japan* (Charles E. Tuttle Co. Rutland Vermont, U.S.A. and Tokyo, 1963).

JANHEINZ JAHN, *Muntu: An Outline of Neo-African Culture* (Faber and Faber, 1961).

HAROLD ISAACS, *The New World of Negro Americans* (The John Day Co., New York, 1963).

ALBERT HOURANI, *Arabic Thought in the Liberal Age 1789-1939* (Oxford University Press, 1962).

D. C. VIJAYAVARDHANA, *The Revolt in the Temple* (Sinha Publications, 1953) obtainable from the Lake Publishing House, Colombo, Ceylon.

KAMEL HUSSEIN, *City of Wrong: A Friday in Jerusalem* (Djambatan, Amsterdam, 1959).

GEORGE ANTONIUS, *The Arab Awakening* (Hamish Hamilton, 1938).

NDABANINGI SITHOLE, *African Nationalism* (Oxford University Press, 1959).

W. MACMAHON BALL, *Nationalism and Communism in East Asia* (Melbourne University Press, and Cambridge University Press, 1952).

JAMES S. COLEMAN, *Nigeria: Background to Nationalism* (University of California Press, 1958).

WALTER Z. LAQUEUR, *Communism and Nationalism in the Middle East* (Routledge and Kegan Paul, 1956).

7 · The Origins of the Ecumenical Movement

S. L. GREENSLADE, *Schism in the Early Church* (S.C.M. Press, 1953).

RUTH ROUSE and STEPHEN CHARLES NEILL, eds., *A History of the Ecumenical Movement, 1517-1948* (S.P.C.K., 1954)

A. J. LEWIS, *Zinzendorf the Ecumenical Pioneer* (S.C.M. Press, 1962).

JOHN S. MOIR, *Church and State in Canada West: Three Studies in the Relationship of Denominationalism and Nationalism, 1841-1867* (University of Toronto Press, 1959).

R. PIERCE BEAVER, *Ecumenical Beginnings in Protestant World Mission—A History of Comity* (Thomas Nelson and Sons, New York, 1962).

W. H. T. GAIRDNER, *Edinburgh 1910: an Account and Interpretation of the World Missionary Conference* (Oliphant, Anderson and Ferrier, 1910).

NORMAN GOODALL, *The Ecumenical Movement: What It Is and What It Does* (Oxford University Press, 1961).

HENRY P. VAN DUSEN, *One Great Ground of Hope: Christian Mission and Christian Unity* (Lutterworth Press, 1961).

KEITH R. BRIDSTON and WALTER D. WAGONER, eds., *Unity in Mid-Career: an Ecumenical Critique* (Collier-Macmillan Ltd., London, 1963).

HANS KÜNG, *The Council and Reunion* (Sheed and Ward, 1961).

ALEXANDER C. ZABRISKIE, *Bishop Brent: Crusader for Christian Unity* (Westminster Press, Philadelphia, 1948).

STEPHEN NEILL, *Men of Unity* (S.C.M. Press, 1960).

P. GARDNER SMITH, ed., *The Roads Converge: A Contribution to the Question of Church Reunion* (Edward Arnold, 1963).

F. B. WELBOURN, *East African Rebels* (S.C.M. Press, 1961).

BENGT G. M. SUNDKLER, *Bantu Prophets in South Africa* (Oxford University Press, 1961).

DOUGLAS WEBSTER, *Pentecostalism and Speaking With Tongues* (Highway Press, 1965).

8 · *Christian Missions in the Contemporary Revolution*

PAUL A. VARG, *Missionaries, Chinese and Diplomats: The American Protestant Missionary Movement in China* (Princeton University Press, 1958).

SEMAINE DE MISSIOLOGIE LOUVAIN, 1956, *Masses Urbaines et Missions* (Desclée de Brouwer, 1957).

S. C. NEILL, *A History of Christian Missions* (Penguin Books, 1964).

RITCHIE CALDER, *Men Against the Jungle* (Allen and Unwin, 1954).

K. M. PANIKKAR, *Asia and Western Dominance* (Allen and Unwin, 1953).

HENDRIK KRAEMER, *Religion and the Christian Faith* (Lutterworth Press, 1956).

R. VOILLAUME, *Seeds of the Desert: The Legacy of Charles de Foucauld* (Burns and Oates, 1955).

C. F. D. MOULE, *The Meaning of Hope* (Highway Press, 1955).

MIRCEA ELIADE, *Myths, Dreams and Mysteries* (Harvill Press, 1960).

MIRCEA ELIADE, *Images and Symbols* (Harvill Press, 1961).

MIRCEA ELIADE, *The Myth of the Eternal Return* (Bollingen Foundation Inc., New York, 1954).

MIRCEA ELIADE, *Patterns in Comparative Religion* (Sheed and Ward, 1958).

R. C. ZAEHNER, *At Sundry Times: An Essay in the Comparison of Religions* (Faber and Faber, 1958).

R. C. ZAEHNER, *The Convergent Spirit: Towards a Dialectics of Religion* (Routledge and Kegan Paul, 1963).

TEILHARD DE CHARDIN, *Letters from a Traveller* (Collins 1962).

A. KENNETH CRAGG, *The Call of the Minaret* (Oxford University Press, 1959).

J. V. TAYLOR, *The Primal Vision: Christian Presence amid African Religion* (S.C.M. Press, 1959).

DOUGLAS WEBSTER, *Pentecostalism and Speaking with Tongues* (Highway Press, 1965).

INDEX OF NAMES